Instant jQuery Boilerplate for Plugins

Get started with jQuery plugin development
with this rapid-paced guide

Jonathan Fielding

PUBLISHING

BIRMINGHAM - MUMBAI

Instant jQuery Boilerplate for Plugins

First published: August 2013

Production Reference: 1170813

Published by Packt Publishing Ltd.
Livery Place
35 Livery Street
Birmingham B3 2PB, UK.

ISBN 978-1-84951-970-0

www.packtpub.com

Credits

Author
Jonathan Fielding

Reviewer
Marcello di Simone

Acquisition Editor
James Jones

Commissioning Editor
Shreerang Deshpande

Technical Editors
Anita Nayak

Sonali S. Vernekar

Copy Editors
Brandt T. D'Mello

Gladson Monteiro

Alfida Paiva

Laxmi Subramanian

Project Coordinator
Suraj Bist

Proofreader
Stephen Copestake

Production Coordinator
Conidon Miranda

Cover Work
Conidon Miranda

About the Author

Jonathan Fielding attended the University of Hull where he studied Internet computing. Since completing his degree, he has worked for a variety of companies across banking and marketing fields, developing both frontend and backend systems.

Jonathan currently works for McCormack & Morrison, a digital agency based in London, UK, developing responsive websites for clients that include Virgin Active, Nyetimber, and Intent Media.

As a regular contributor to open source, he has launched several of his own open source projects, including several jQuery plugins, and regularly publishes tutorials on his blog with the aim of sharing knowledge.

I would like to thank my wife, Charlie, and my two fantastic children for supporting me while I have been writing this book.

About the Reviewer

Marcello di Simone is a senior web developer with a strong focus on frontend technologies (such as JavaScript, Node.js, HTML, and CSS) and is currently developing native mobile games for Android at Innogames GmbH in his adopted home, Hamburg, Germany.

www.PacktPub.com

Support files, eBooks, discount offers and more

You might want to visit www.PacktPub.com for support files and downloads related to your book.

Did you know that Packt offers eBook versions of every book published, with PDF and ePub files available? You can upgrade to the eBook version at www.PacktPub.com and, as a print book customer, you are entitled to a discount on the eBook copy. Get in touch with us at service@packtpub.com for more details.

At www.PacktPub.com, you can also read a collection of free technical articles, sign up for a range of free newsletters and receive exclusive discounts and offers on Packt books and eBooks.

http://PacktLib.PacktPub.com

Do you need instant solutions to your IT questions? PacktLib is Packt's online digital book library. Here, you can access, read and search across Packt's entire library of books.

Why Subscribe?

- ▸ Fully searchable across every book published by Packt
- ▸ Copy-and-paste, print and bookmark content
- ▸ On-demand and accessible via web browsers

Free Access for Packt account holders

If you have an account with Packt at www.PacktPub.com, you can use this to access PacktLib today and view nine entirely free books. Simply use your login credentials for immediate access.

Table of Contents

Preface

Instant jQuery Boilerplate for Plugins is a guide to getting started with writing your first jQuery plugin. We will explore the different options available, offer a full breakdown of what jQuery Boilerplate has to offer, and then go through several tutorials to get you comfortable with writing a plugin. Once you have got to grips with writing your plugin, we will finally explore how you can go about making your own plugin and making it available as an open source project.

What this book covers

Getting started with jQuery plugins (Simple) explores the steps we need to take to prepare ourselves for jQuery plugin development using jQuery Boilerplate.

Getting started with your first plugin (Simple) will get us started with writing our first plugin. We will write a simple plugin that swaps the shape that is shown on the page.

Creating a simple JSON reader (Simple) looks at creating a JSON reader that reads your tweets from Twitter and displays them on the page.

jQuery Hover panels with jQuery Boilerplate (Simple) explores creating a plugin that allows users to hover over a panel to reveal alternative content.

Writing a carousel with jQuery Boilerplate (Intermediate) explores how we go about writing a carousel jQuery plugin.

AJAX bookshelves with jQuery Boilerplate (Advanced) explains how to build an AJAX bookshelf that imports a JSON feed and then builds the HTML to create a pull-out bookshelf.

Writing a validation plugin using jQuery Boilerplate (Intermediate) explains how to write a validation plugin; once we have finished our plugin, we will learn how we can test it using QUnit.

Who this book is for

This book is for anyone who wants to write their own plugin or know the basics of plugin writing so that they can contribute to other plugins. You need to have a good understanding of HTML, CSS, JavaScript and preferably have used the jQuery library before.

When writing this book, it is assumed that readers have a good understanding of:

► HTML

► CSS

► JavaScript

► jQuery

If you wish to do some reading on jQuery before you begin to develop your own plugins, I recommend the following book:

Learning JQuery Third Edition by *Jonathan Chaffer* and *Karl Swedberg, Packt Publishing*

Conventions

In this book, you will find a number of styles of text that distinguish between different kinds of information. Here are some examples of these styles and an explanation of their meaning.

Code words in text, database table names, folder names, filenames, file extensions, pathnames, dummy URLs, user input, and Twitter handles are shown as follows: "Using our base template from earlier, we will start out with creating a new file called data.json in the root of the project."

A block of code is set as follows:

```
var templates = {
        container    : "<div id='bookshelf'><h1>%BookshelfName%</h1><a
        class='pull' href='#'>Pull</a><div
        id='bookshelf_books'></div></div>",
        book: "<div class='book'><h2>%Title%</h2><img
        src='%Cover%'/><p>%Author%</p><p>%Publisher%</p></div>"
    };
```

When we wish to draw your attention to a particular part of a code block, the relevant lines or items are set in bold:

```
var templates = {
        container   : "<div id='bookshelf'><h1>%BookshelfName%</h1><a
        class='pull' href='#'>Pull</a><div
        id='bookshelf_books'></div></div>",
        book: "<div class='book'><h2>%Title%</h2><img
        src='%Cover%'/><p>%Author%</p><p>%Publisher%</p></div>"
    };
```

New terms and **important words** are shown in bold. Words that you see on the screen, in menus or dialog boxes, for example, appear in the text like this: "Clicking the **Next** button moves you to the next screen".

> [Warnings or important notes appear in a box like this.]

> [Tips and tricks appear like this.]

Reader feedback

Feedback from our readers is always welcome. Let us know what you think about this book—what you liked or may have disliked. Reader feedback is important for us to develop titles that you really get the most out of.

To send us general feedback, simply send an e-mail to feedback@packtpub.com, and mention the book title via the subject of your message.

If there is a topic that you have expertise in and you are interested in either writing or contributing to a book, see our author guide on www.packtpub.com/authors.

Customer support

Now that you are the proud owner of a Packt book, we have a number of things to help you to get the most from your purchase.

Downloading the example code

You can download the example code files for all Packt books you have purchased from your account at `http://www.packtpub.com`. If you purchased this book elsewhere, you can visit `http://www.packtpub.com/support` and register to have the files e-mailed directly to you.

Errata

Although we have taken every care to ensure the accuracy of our content, mistakes do happen. If you find a mistake in one of our books—maybe a mistake in the text or the code—we would be grateful if you would report this to us. By doing so, you can save other readers from frustration and help us improve subsequent versions of this book. If you find any errata, please report them by visiting `http://www.packtpub.com/submit-errata`, selecting your book, clicking on the **errata submission form** link, and entering the details of your errata. Once your errata are verified, your submission will be accepted and the errata will be uploaded on our website or added to any list of existing errata, under the Errata section of that title. Any existing errata can be viewed by selecting your title from `http://www.packtpub.com/support`.

Piracy

Piracy of copyright material on the Internet is an ongoing problem across all media. At Packt, we take the protection of our copyright and licenses very seriously. If you come across any illegal copies of our works, in any form, on the Internet, please provide us with the location address or website name immediately so that we can pursue a remedy.

Please contact us at `copyright@packtpub.com` with a link to the suspected pirated material.

We appreciate your help in protecting our authors and our ability to bring you valuable content.

Questions

You can contact us at `questions@packtpub.com` if you are having a problem with any aspect of the book, and we will do our best to address it.

Instant jQuery Boilerplate for Plugins

Welcome to *Instant jQuery Boilerplate for Plugins*. One of the most compelling features of jQuery is its vast array of plugins that have been developed for the library. jQuery has supported plugins since its conception and, as such, has led to the creation of many great plugins including ColorBox, Chosen, and Hover Intent. With the ample number of plugins available, it is very easy to save yourself a significant amount of time when building a website by finding a plugin that already does what you want.

Getting started with jQuery plugins (Simple)

When looking at a jQuery plugin in its most basic form, it is a collection of code that we use to add a particular piece of functionality to the website we are building. Almost any piece of functionality on a website could be built as a plugin, from the way the navigation works to the Twitter feed being pulled into the site. This first recipe will guide you on how to get started with jQuery Plugin development by taking you through the step-by-step process of setting up a suitable development environment.

Getting ready

Before we dive into preparing our template, we need to decide upon what exactly we need to include in it. The simplest option we could take is to just download HTML5 Boilerplate and pair it with jQuery Boilerplate; however, it would be an overkill for plugin development as it includes `Modernizr` and `Normalise.css`, which we do not need. The option we will choose instead is to write our own template, which will include only what we need. The benefit of this is that we do not build any dependencies for other JavaScript (other than jQuery) or CSS.

Before we can dive into writing our first plugin, we need to first ensure that we have all the necessary files.

jQuery: While writing this book, the current version of jQuery is 1.10.1; we have opted to use the 1.x branch version of jQuery to maintain support for legacy versions of Internet Explorer.

How to do it

1. Our first step is to prepare the folder structure of our template. We will need a folder for our JavaScript, a folder for any CSS our plugin requires, and a folder for images.

    The folder structure should be as follows:

    - /css
    - /js
    - /images

2. With our folder structure in place, we now need to set up our HTML. We only need something simple: a container, the stylesheet included in the head of the document, and the script files just before the closing tag of the body of the document. The code snippet for setting up HTML is as follows:

    ```html
    <!DOCTYPE html>
    <html>
      <head>
        <title></title>
        <link rel="stylesheet" href="css/main.css">
      </head>
      <body>
        <div class="container">
        </div>
        <script src="js/jquery.js"></script>
        <script src="js/plugin.js"></script>
        <script src="js/main.js"></script>
      </body>
    </html>
    ```

3. Moving on to the main CSS document, we will not be needing a full reset for the purpose of this book; however, we will set the font sizes to sensible values. We are setting the base font size to `62.5%`, so that going forward we can use a base 10 multiplication to work out our font sizes. The reason for resetting the font size for nested elements to `1em` is to stop the issue where we have `1.2em * 1.2em` for an anchor within an `li` or `p` tag. Refer to the following code snippet for this purpose:

    ```css
    body{
      font-size: 62.5%;
    }
    p, li, a{
    ```

```
      font-size: 1.2em;
}
li p, li a, p a{
   font-size: 1em
}
```

4. With our HTML and CSS in place, we will now start to add the JavaScript files we need. Having previously downloaded jQuery, we will need to rename the file to `jquery.js` and place it in the `/js` folder.

5. With jQuery in place, we will now add jQuery Boilerplate to the template. We will do this by creating a `plugins.js` file in the `/js` folder and placing the jQuery Boilerplate code inside. We will be including the version of jQuery Boilerplate without the comments as follows:

```javascript
;(function ( $, window, document, undefined ) {

    var pluginName = "defaultPluginName",
      defaults = {
        propertyName: "value"
      };

    // The actual plugin constructor
    function Plugin( element, options ) {
      this.element = element;
      this.options = $.extend( {}, defaults, options );
      this._defaults = defaults;
      this._name = pluginName;
      this.init();
    }

    Plugin.prototype = {
      init: function() {

      },
      yourOtherFunction: function(el, options) {
      }
    };
    $.fn[pluginName] = function ( options ) {
      return this.each(function () {
        if (!$.data(this, "plugin_" + pluginName)) {
          $.data(this, "plugin_" + pluginName, new Plugin( this,
            options ));
        }
      });
    };

})( jQuery, window, document );
```

6. We also need to include a JavaScript file for instantiating our jQuery plugin; we will name this as `main.js` and place it in the `\js` directory. Inside this file we will include an **Immediately Invoked Function Expression (IIFE)** to wrap in our code to ensure that there is no leaking into the global namespace.

```
(function(){
}());
```

Downloading the example code

You can download the example code files for all Packt books you have purchased from your account at `http://www.packtpub.com`. If you purchased this book elsewhere, you can visit `http://www.packtpub.com/support` and register to have the files e-mailed directly to you.

There's more

Before you begin writing your first plugin, it is important to ensure that you are aware of the best coding practices you should endeavor to follow.

There are several key best practices for building jQuery plugins as follows:

Wrapping your plugin in a closure

The primary reason that you should be wrapping your plugin in a closure is to ensure that your code is self containing and that you do not pollute the namespace by accidently creating global variables. When we declare our wrapper closure, we can also pass the no conflicts jQuery through our plugin instead of $, and declare $ as a parameter that is passed to our plugin. This ensures we can still use the $ function we are familiar with inside our plugin, and even outside our plugin if the site is using jQuery in the **no conflicts** mode.

Passing settings as an object literal

One of the great things about a flexible plugin is that it allows its users to set different options depending on how they wish to use the plugin.

The best-practice approach would be to use an object literal to pass your plugin options. The benefit is that the users are then able to change as many settings as they want without it being affected by the order they are inputted in. An example of how this would work is as follows:

```
$('body').demoPlugin({ "example":"different"});
```

In this case, we would only have to pass one argument to the function. The benefit of this approach is that it also allows us to easily define default values in the plugin, which can be overridden by the user's options. Within our plugin, the `defaults` and `options` objects are merged with the `$.extends` method of jQuery, which along with the user values replaces the default values.

Claiming only one namespace

When you are developing a plugin, it is important to not clutter up the $.fn namespace by claiming more than one namespace. The main reason for this is that if your plugin takes up several namespace names on the $.fn object, you have a higher chance that you will have conflicts with other plugins. If you want to expose several plugin methods, the recommended way is to store all your methods in an object literal and to call them by passing the string name of the method to the plugin. When working with jQuery Boilerplate, we need to extend the plugin wrapper to enable it to expose several plugin methods; we can do this by adding a simple `if` statement to check whether an `options` object or a method name has been passed by the user.

```
$.fn[pluginName] = function ( options, methodOptions) {
    var localPlugin = null;

    if (options === undefined || typeof options === 'object') {
      return this.each(function () {
        if (!$.data(this, "plugin_" + pluginName)) {
          $.data(this, "plugin_" + pluginName, new Plugin( this,
            options ));
        }
      });
    }
    else if(options === "otherMethod"){
      //call other method here
    }
};
```

Always returning this

One of the things that makes jQuery popular is its ability to chain operations, which is achieved through chainable functions returning `this`. To ensure your plugin does not break this functionality, it is important that you return `this`.

One of the most common ways in which plugins return `this` is by using `return this.each()`. This uses the `jQuery.each()` function to loop through each of the elements that have been passed to the plugin, which will then do something with each of these elements. As per the rule of always returning `this`, the `jQuery.each()` function will also return `this` therefore returning `this.each()`, which is the same as returning `this`.

Unlike the other best practices, there is one exception to this rule. In a situation where you need to return a value, you are able to return the value instead of `this`.

Getting started with your first plugin (Simple)

Having already set up a template for creating jQuery Plugins using jQuery Boilerplate, we are now able to progress to writing our first plugin. For this recipe, we will look at how we can create a plugin that manipulates the shape of a `div` element.

We will achieve this by writing some HTML to declare a shape and a button, declaring each shape in the CSS, and then using the JavaScript to toggle which shape is shown by toggling the CSS class appended to it. Writing this plugin should help you familiarize yourself both with jQuery plugin development and the jQuery Boilerplate template.

Getting ready

Before we dive into our development, we need to have a good idea of how our plugin is going to work. For this, we will write some simple HTML to declare a shape and a button. Each shape will be declared in the CSS, and then we will use the JavaScript to toggle which shape is shown by toggling the CSS class appended to it. The aim of this recipe is to help you familiarize yourself both with jQuery plugin development and the jQuery Boilerplate template.

For this recipe, we will use a copy of the template we created in the previous recipe.

How to do it

1. Our first step is to set up our HTML. For this we need to open up our `index.html` file. We will need to add two elements in HTML: `shape` and `wrapper` to contain our shape. The button for changing the `shape` element will be added dynamically by our JavaScript. We will then add an event listener to it so that we can change the shape. The HTML code for this is as follows:

    ```
    <div class="shape_wrapper">
    <div class="shape">
    </div>
    </div>
    ```

    This should be placed in the `div` tag with `class="container"` in our `index.html` file.

2. We then need to define each of the shapes we intend to use using CSS. In this example, we will draw a square, a circle, a triangle, and an oval, all of which can be defined using CSS. The shape we will be manipulating will be `100px * 100px`. The following CSS should be placed in your `main.css` file:

    ```
    .shape{
      width: 100px;
      height: 100px;
    ```

```
    background: #ff0000;
    margin: 10px 0px;
  }
  .shape.circle{
    border-radius: 50px;
  }
  .shape.triangle{
    width: 0;
    height: 0;
    background: transparent;
    border-left: 50px solid transparent;
    border-right: 50px solid transparent;
    border-bottom: 100px solid #ff0000;
  }
  .shape.oval{
    width: 100px;
    height: 50px;
    margin: 35px 0;
    border-radius: 50px / 25px;
  }
```

3. Now it's time to get onto the JavaScript. The first step in creating the plugin is to name it; in this case we will call it `shapeShift`. In the jQuery Boilerplate code, we will need to set the value of the `pluginName` variable to equal `shapeShift`. This is done as:

```
var pluginName = "shapeShift"
```

4. Once we have named the plugin, we can edit our `main.js` file to call the plugin. We will call the plugin by selecting the element using jQuery and creating an instance of our plugin by running `.shapeShift()`; as follows:

```
(function(){
  $('.shape_wrapper').shapeShift();
}());
```

    For now this will do nothing, but it will enable us to test our plugin once we have written the code.

5. To ensure the flexibility of our plugin, we will store our shapes as part of the `defaults` object literal, meaning that, in the future, the shapes used by the plugin can be changed without the plugin code being changed. We will also set the class name of the shape in the defaults object literal so that this can be chosen by the plugin user as well. After doing this, your defaults object should look like the following:

```
defaults = {
    shapes: ["square", "circle", "triangle", "oval"],
    shapeClass: ".shape"
};
```

6. When the `.shapeShift()` function is triggered, it will create an instance of our plugin and then fire the `init` function. For this instance of our plugin, we will store the current shape location in the array; this is done by adding it to `this` by using `this.shapeRef = 0`. The reason we are storing the shape reference on `this` is that it attaches it to this instance of the plugin, and it will not be available to other instances of the same plugin on the same page.

7. Once we have stored the `shape` reference, we need to apply the first `shape` class to the `div` element according to our shape. The simplest way to do this is to use jQuery to get the shape and then use `addClass` to add the shape class as follows:

```
$(this.element).find(this.options.shapeClass).addClass(this.
options.shapes[this.shapeRef]);
```

8. The final step that we need to do in our `init` function is to add our button to enable the user to change the shape. To do this, we simply append a button element to the shape container as follows:

```
$(this.element).append('<button>Change Shape</button>');
```

9. Once we have our `button` element, we then need to add the `shape` reference, which changes the shape of the elements. To do this we will create a separate function called `changeShape`. While we are still in our `init` function, we can add an event handler to call the `changeShape` function onto the button. For reasons that will become apparent shortly, we will use the event delegation format of the `jQuery.on()` function to do this:

```
$(this.element).on('click','button',this.changeShape);
```

10. We now need to create our `changeShape` function; previously we saw that jQuery Boilerplate includes a function called `yourOtherFunction`; the first thing we will do is change this function name to `changeShape`. We will then change the function declaration to accept a parameter, in this case `e`.

The first thing to note is that this function is called from an event listener on a DOM element and therefore `this` is actually the element that has been clicked on. As previously mentioned, this function was called using event delegation; the reason for this becomes apparent here as it allows us to find out which instance of the plugin belongs to the button that has been clicked on. We do this by using the `e` parameter that was passed to the function. The `e` parameter passed to the function is the jQuery event object related to the `click` event that has been fired. Inside it, we will find a reference to the original element that the `click` event was set to, which in this case is the element that the instance of the plugin is tied to. To retrieve the instance of the plugin, we can simply use the `jQuery.data()` function. The instance of the plugin is stored on the element as data using the data key plugin_pluginName, so we are able to retrieve it the same way as follows:

```
var plugin = $(e.delegateTarget).data("plugin_" +
pluginName);
```

11. Now that we have the plugin instance, we are able to access everything it contains; the first thing we need to do is to remove the current `shape` class from the `shape` element in the DOM. To do this, we will simply find the `shape` element then look up in the `shapes` array to get the currently displayed `shape`, and then use the `jQuery.removeClass` function to remove the individual class.

    The code for doing this starts with a simple jQuery selector that allows us to work with the plugin element; we do this using `$(plugin.element)`. We then look inside the plugin element to find the actual shape. As the name of the shape class is configurable, we can read this from our plugin option; so when we are finding the shape we use `.find(plugin.options.shapeClass)`. Finally we add the class; so that we know which shape is next, we look up the shape class from the `shapes` array stored in the plugin options, selecting the item indicated by the `plugin.shapeRef`. The full command then looks as follows:

    ```
    $(plugin.element).find(plugin.options.shapeClass).
    removeClass(plugin.options.shapes[plugin.shapeRef]);
    ```

12. We then need to work out which is the next shape we should show; we know that the current `shape` reference can be found in `plugin.shapeRef`, so we just need to work out if we have any more shapes left in the `shape` array or if we should start from the beginning. To do this, we look at the value of `plugin.shapeRef` and compare it to the length of the `shapes` array minus 1 (we substract 1 because arrays start at 0); if the `shape` reference is equal to the length of the `shapes` array minus 1, we know that we have reached the last shape, so we reset the `plugin.shapeRef` parameter to 0. Otherwise, we simply increment the `shapeRef` parameter by 1 as shown in the snippet:

    ```
    if((plugin.shapeRef) === (plugin.options.shapes.length -1)){
            plugin.shapeRef = 0;
    }
    else{
            plugin.shapeRef = plugin.shapeRef+1;
    }
    ```

13. Our final step is to add the new `shape` class to the `shape` element; this can be achieved by finding the `shape` element and using the `jQuery.addClass` function to add the shape from the `shapes` array. This is very similar to our `removeClass` command that we used earlier with `addClass` replacing `removeClass`.

    ```
    $(plugin.element).find(plugin.options.shapeClass).addClass(plugin.
    options.shapes[plugin.shapeRef]);
    ```

14. At this point we should now have a working plugin; so if we fire up the browser and navigate to the `index.html` file, we should get a square with a button beneath it. Clicking on the button should show the next shape. If your code is working correctly, the shapes should be shown in the order: square, circle, triangle, oval, and then loop back to square.

15. As a final test to show that each plugin instance is tied to one element, we will add a second element to the page. This is as simple as duplicating the original `shape_wrapper` and creating a second one as shown:

```
<div class="shape_wrapper">
        <div class="shape">
        </div>
</div>
```

16. If everything is working correctly when loading the `index.html` page, we will have 2 squares each with a button underneath them, and on clicking the button only the shape above will change.

Creating a simple JSON reader (Simple)

Now that we have learnt the basics of writing a plugin, we will look at how to write a plugin that can read and process data provided by a JSON feed. For this example, we will be using a feed provided by Twitter for all of our recent tweets.

Getting ready

In preparation for writing this plugin, we need to have a good idea of how our JSON reader plugin is going to work. The JSON reader will work by loading the Twitter feed for a particular user from the Twitter REST API. Version 1.1 of the Twitter REST API requires you to authenticate to retrieve tweets so we will use **Yahoo Query Language** (**YQL**) to retrieve the tweets. The plugin will then need to loop through each of the individual posts from the user's Twitter feed, building the HTML required for each tweet. This will then need to be appended to the page.

For this recipe we will use a copy of the template we created in the previous recipe.

How to do it

1. Before we start coding we need to first create a Twitter application; we can do this by visiting `https://dev.twitter.com/apps/new` and filling out the form. Upon registration of your Twitter application, you will be taken to the information screen, which looks like the one in the following screenshot:

If you scroll down to the bottom of the page you will see a section entitled **Your Access Token**; within this section is a button entitled **Create my access token**. Click on this button to generate the keys you will need to authenticate the app.

You will need to make a note of the values for **Consumer key**, **Consumer secret**, **Access token**, and **Access token secret** for use in our plugin.

We can now get on with coding. The first thing to do is to set up our basic HTML template. All we will need is a simple container to output our Twitter feed to. Because the feed will not load for people without JavaScript, it is good to include a `noscript` tag letting your users know they will need to enable JavaScript to see your Twitter feed.

```
<div class="feed">
  <noscript>Showing the twitter feed requires
    javascript</noscript>
</div>
```

2. Our next step is to set up the call to our plugin so we are able to test it as we go along; we will be naming our plugin `getTwitterFeed` and will need to pass our feed element to the plugin. We will need to pass the authentication information that we had set up prior to the plugin so that it can authenticate with the Twitter API. This is done as follows:

```
(function(){
  $('.feed').getTwitterFeed({
    consumer_key: "hgp2uG7P2mQYMk7XO7C1xg",
    consumer_secret:
      "gQhikjacpPGIavnobjZHDhWtbYvhwUZj2XWk0gfMrZQ",
    access_token:
      "255939300-6pTHJaW1iWEOAMWS9cjQcFvNSm7q5BzUQXfLQIBS",
    access_token_secret:
      "fOxKBfvjvSpuuPrsAp0xQzOMfWRXeR5yLC9Jcimoo"
  });
}());
```

3. We will name our plugin `getTwitterFeed`, which is set as the value of the `pluginName` variable. We then need to add some default options to the plugin. For a simple plugin that gets the JSON feed of a Twitter user, we will need to know the username of the user we want to get the tweets from. We will need to pass the Twitter authentication details we had set up prior to the plugin. We might also want to add the option to configure the number of tweets we want to get and whether we want to show retweets in that list. We will add all these options into our `defaults` options object literal.

```
var pluginName = "getTwitterFeed",
  defaults = {
    user: "JonthanFielding",
    consumer_key: "",
    consumer_secret: "",
    access_token: "",
    access_token_secret: "",
    count: "10"
  }
```

4. We then need to store the API URL in a variable; the official API we are going to use is documented fully at `https://dev.twitter.com/docs/api/1.1/ get/statuses/user_timeline`. To enable us to authenticate with the API, we will use YQL. The API we will therefore be using is `https://query. yahooapis.com/v1/public/yql?q=%20SELECT%20*%20FROM%20twitter. statuses.user_timeline%20WHERE%20consumer_key%3D%22CONSUMER_ KEY%22%20and%20consumer_secret%3D%22CONSUMER_SECRET%22%20 and%20access_token%3D%22ACCESS_TOKEN%22%20and%20 access_token_secret%3D%22ACCESS_TOKEN_SECRET%22%20and%20 count%3D%22COUNT%22%20and%20screen_name%3D%22SCREEN_NAME%22&fo rmat=json&env=store%3A%2F%2Fdatatables.org%2Falltableswithkeys`. We will need to call the URL with a callback parameter so that the browser will fire a callback upon successfully retrieving the Twitter feed. This callback parameter is added by adding `callback=?` to the URL. We will need to ensure our plugin can update the authentication, screen name, and tweet count value found in the URL.

```
baseFeedURL = "
https://query.yahooapis.com/v1/public/yql?callback=?&q=%20
SELECT%20*%20FROM%20twitter.statuses.user_timeline%20
WHERE%20consumer_key%3D%22{CONKEY}%22%20and%20consumer_
secret%3D%22{CONSEC}%22%20and%20access_token%3D%22{ACCTOK}%22%20
and%20access_token_secret%3D%22{ACCSEC}%22%20and%20
count%3D%22{COUNT}%22%20and%20screen_name%3D%22{USER}%22&format=js
on&env=store%3A%2F%2Fdatatables.org%2Falltableswithkeys";
```

5. The plugin constructor will not need any changes, so we can start working on our `init` method.

   The first step in our `init` method is to build the feed URL; when building the feed URL, we will store the URL on the plugin instance as `this.feedURL`. The URL we stored in the `baseFeedURL` variable has placeholders for each of the values for consumer key (`{CONKEY}`), consumer secret (`{CONSEC}`), access token (`{ACCTOK}`), access token secret (`{ACCSEC}`), Twitter name (`{User}`), and Tweet count (`{COUNT}`). For these values we will simply use `.replace` to replace the placeholder with the correct value from the options. The final code for building the feed URL is:

   ```
   this.feedURL = baseFeedURL.replace('{CONKEY}',
       this.options.consumer_key);
   this.feedURL = this.feedURL.replace('{CONSEC}',
       this.options.consumer_secret);
   this.feedURL = this.feedURL.replace('{ACCTOK}',
       this.options.access_token);
   this.feedURL = this.feedURL.replace('{ACCSEC}',
       this.options.access_token_secret);
   this.feedURL = this.feedURL.replace('{COUNT}',
       this.options.count);
   this.feedURL = this.feedURL.replace('{USER}',
       this.options.user);
   ```

6. With this URL we now need to retrieve the JSON feed. Thankfully, jQuery makes this really easy for us with a simple function called `$.getJSON`. `$.getJSON` will get the JSON feed and pass the resulting JSON object to the function we specify. When we fire the `$.getJSON` function, we need to pass it two parameters, firstly the JSON feed and secondly the `return` function.

   ```
   $.getJSON(this.feedURL, $.proxy(this.updateFeed, this));
   ```

   As you will notice in our code, we are using `$.proxy` to handle our `return` function. The reason for this is that we want to ensure we maintain access to the plugin instance through the use of `this`. Without the `$.proxy` function, the new function that receives our JSON data will instead have a `this` reference from the context of the JSON feed rather than from the plugin instance. To use `$.proxy`, we are passing it our method for outputting the feed and the plugin instance (as `this`).

7. Now on to our `updateFeed` method; we need to add this to our `Plugin.` `prototype` object literal. This method needs to take one parameter; in this case, we will call it `data`.

```
Plugin.prototype = {
    init: function() {
    },
    updateFeed: function(data) {

    }
};
```

8. Now that we have our `updateFeed` method, we can write a simple line of code that will allow us to test whether the JSON feed is coming in correctly. This is a simple `console.log(data)` inside our `updateFeed` method and should output the returned JSON from Twitter. The full `updateFeed` function should look like this:

```
updateFeed: function(data) {
    console.log(data);
}
```

When testing this in our browser, the resulting array of objects should look like this:

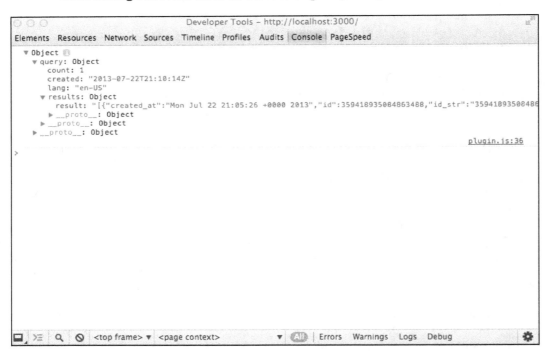

If we get an Object in the console similar to those shown in the preceding screenshot, the plugin is working as expected so far. We now need to look at outputting this to the browser.

As you may have noticed, the results shown in our console were nested in a JSON object; however, the actual results are stored as a string. To be able to output our tweets, we will need to parse the string to JSON using $.parseJSON.

```
updateFeed: function(data) {
  var feedData =
    jQuery.parseJSON(data.query.results.result);
}
```

9. We then need to get the element that we will add our tweets to by storing $(this.element) in a variable.

```
var $feed = $(this.element);
```

10. We then need to loop through the array to output the tweets one at a time. The simplest way to do this is to use the jQuery.each() function to loop through the array so we can process each tweet one at a time.

    Inside our loop we want to get the text from each of the tweets; we will build up our new tweet HTML by adding to it a variable called newTweet. We will then append the newTweet variable to the element. When using jQuery.each(), the particular item we are currently accessing can be accessed via this, so our tweet text is retrieved using this.text.

```
$(feedData).each(function(){
    var newTweet = '<div class="tweet">';
    newTweet += this.text;
    newTweet += '</div>';
    $feed.append(newTweet);
});
```

By refreshing the browser, we can now see the tweets outputted by our plugin.

11. If we want to have multiple feeds on the page, we can change our HTML so that we have several feed containers. One suggested way to do this is by adding a second class to each feed container with a unique identifier. The simplest idea would be to name the class by the name of the Twitter user. In this case we would have two containers, one with the class jonthanfielding and another with the Twitter username of one of my favorite developers, paul_irish. The resulting containers would be:

```
<div class="feed" id="jonthanfielding">
  <noscript>Showing the twitter feed requires
    javascript</noscript>
</div>
```

```
<div class="feed" id="paulirish">
  <noscript>Showing the twitter feed requires
    javascript</noscript>
</div>
```

12. We then need to change our JavaScript file to populate both the feeds. Our first call to the plugin remains mostly the same; however, we need to change the element to target only the first feed container. The original `$('.feed').getTwitterFeed(OPTIONS)` will become `$('#jonthanfielding').getTwitterFeed(OPTIONS)`.

    The second feed requires us to set the `username` to the Twitter username of Paul Irish. The original `$('.feed').getTwitterFeed()` would become `$('#paulirish).getTwitterFeed({"user":"paul_irish", OTHER_OPTIONS})`. The final code for this would be:

```
(function(){
  $('#jonthanfielding').getTwitterFeed({
    consumer_key: "hgp2uG7P2mQYMk7BO7C1xg",
    consumer_secret:
      "gQhikjacpPGIavnobjZHDhWtbYvhwUZj2NWk0gfMrZQ",
    access_token:
      "255939300-6pTHJaW1iWEOAMWS9cjQcFvNSm7q5BzUQ0fLQIBS",
    access_token_secret:
      "fOxKBfvjvSpuuPrsAp0xQzOMfWRHeR5yLC9Jcimoo"
  });
  $('#paulirish').getTwitterFeed({
    "user":"paul_irish",
    consumer_key: "hgp2uG7P2mQYMk7BO7C1xg",
    consumer_secret:
      "gQhikjacpPGIavnobjZHDhWtbYvhwUZj2NWk0gfMrZQ",
    access_token:
      "255939300-6pTHJaW1iWEOAMWS9cjQcFvNSm7q5BzUQ0fLQIBS",
    access_token_secret:
      "fOxKBfvjvSpuuPrsAp0xQzOMfWRHeR5yLC9Jcimoo"
  });
}());
```

jQuery Hover panels with jQuery Boilerplate (Simple)

Hover panels are becoming increasingly popular on websites with the default starting content being replaced with alternative content on hover, usually with an animation for the transition between the two pieces of content. For this task we are going to create such a plugin. To transition between the two pieces of content, we will simply hide the default content and show the hover content.

Getting Ready

We will once again use the template, which we had previously set up.

How to do it...

1. Our first step is to make our HTML ready. All our panels need to be encapsulated within a container; in our case, we will call our container `hoverpanels`:

```
<div class="hoverpanels">
</div>
```

2. Then we need to define our panels; each panel needs a title, some default content, and then some content that we will show when the website user hovers over the panel.

```
<div class="panel">
  <h1>Panel 1</h1>
  <div class="default">
    <p>Lorem ipsum dolor sit amet, consectetur adipiscing
    elit. Suspendisse sit amet felis dolor, et porttitor
    sapien. Vestibulum leo velit, bibendum auctor commodo
    sed, fermentum a eros. In at lorem a ante faucibus
    luctus. Sed dapibus volutpat neque, et facilisis
    mauris.</p>
  </div>
```

```
<div class="hover">
  <ul>
    <li><a href="#">Test Link 1</a></li>
    <li><a href="#">Test Link 2</a></li>
    <li><a href="#">Test Link 3</a></li>
    <li><a href="#">Test Link 4</a></li>
  </ul>
</div>
</div>
```

3. While we are developing this plugin, it is useful to have multiple panels as this will allow us to see how multiple panels will work together; thus, we will simply duplicate the panel three times inside the `div` class's `hoverpanels`.

4. Now that we have prepared our HTML, we will define the CSS to set a width for the `hoverpanels` container; we will set this to `666px` (as this allows our panels to be `222px` wide).

```
.hoverpanels{
  width:666px;
  overflow: hidden;
}
```

5. We now need to define the CSS for our individual panels. For visual purposes, it makes sense to add a border, width, padding, and background; however, these do not have a major influence on the plugin. To ensure that they are all in one line in the `hoverpanels` container, we need to add `float: left`. As we want all of them to stay at the same height, it makes sense to add a `min-height` value as well. Also, for visual reasons, we will also set font sizes on the `h1`, `p`, and `li` tags.

```
.panel{
  border:1px solid #000000;
  width:200px;
  float:left;
  padding:10px;
  min-height:220px;
  background:#ccc;
}

.panel p, .panel li{
  font-size: 1.3em;
}

.panel h1{
  font-size: 1.5em;
}
```

6. Now that we have our CSS complete, we can start working on our plugin. Our first step is to set the plugin name, which we shall set as `hoverpanels`, as shown:

```
var pluginName = "hoverpanels"
```

7. We also need to set up the plugin defaults. For the hover panel's plugin, we will need to set default values for our default selector, the hover content selector, and the level to which we will fade our unhovered items, which is done as follows:

```
defaults = {
  defaultContent: '.default',
  hoverContent: '.hover',
  fadeLevel: '0.5'
};
```

8. We then want to set up our methods. It is important that we separate the initialization logic from the user action logic. We already have the `init` method; however, we also want to add a method to handle the website user's actions. We will simply call this method `action` and add it to the `Plugin` prototype, as shown:

```
Plugin.prototype = {
  init: function() {
  },
  action: function(e){
  }
};
```

9. Getting started with the `init` method, we need to start with caching the element as `$element`. The reason for caching this is so that we only have to do the lookup once using jQuery.

```
init: function() {
    var $element = $(this.element);
},
```

10. Using our cached `$element` variable, we now need to hide the hover content. We can use the `jQuery.find()` method to find the hover content within the hover panels container. The following is a code snippet for this purpose:

```
init: function() {
  var $element = $(this.element);
  $element.find(this.options.hoverContent).hide();
},
```

11. Next, we need to add our `mouseenter` and `mouseleave` events to the plugin. Rather than adding the event listeners directly to each of the individual panels, we are going to add the event listener to the container that we have cached as `$element`. The aim of this is to optimize the performance of the plugin by minimizing the number of event listeners that each instance of the plugin adds.

1. The first event listener that we need to add to the `$element` variable is the `mouseenter` event, using `this.action`, which is done as follows:

```
init: function() {
  var $element = $(this.element);
  $element.find(this.options.hoverContent).hide();
  $element.on('mouseenter', '.panel', this.action);
},
```

2. The second event listener we need to add to the `$element` variable is the `mouseleave` event, again using `this.action`, which is done as follows:

```
init: function() {
  var $element = $(this.element);
  $element.find(this.options.hoverContent).hide();
  $element.on('mouseenter', '.panel', this.action);
  $element.on('mouseleave', '.panel', this.action);
},
```

12. We have now finished writing our initialization logic, so we can now move on to working on the `action` method. The first thing to do is to access the instance of the plugin by retrieving it using the `jQuery.data()` method. We also need to retrieve the current action from `e.type`, which we will store in the `activeEvent` variable as follows:

```
action: function(e){
  var plugin = $(e.delegateTarget).data("plugin_" + pluginName),
  activeEvent = e.type;
}
```

13. Next, we need to write an `if` statement to determine whether the action is `mouseenter` or `mouseleave` so that we know which functionality is needed. The code snippet for this is as follows:

```
action: function(e){
  var plugin = $(e.delegateTarget).data("plugin_" +
    pluginName),
  activeEvent = e.type,
  $this = $(this);

  if(activeEvent === "mouseenter"){
  }
  else if(activeEvent === "mouseleave"){
  }
}
```

14. If the `activeEvent` variable is `mouseenter`, we will first hide the default content using the `jQuery.hide()` method. We will then show the hover content using the `jQuery.show()` method. The code snippet for this is as follows:

```
action: function(e){
  var plugin = $(e.delegateTarget).data("plugin_" +
    pluginName),
  activeEvent = e.type,
  $this = $(this);
;

  if(activeEvent === "mouseenter"){
    $this.find(plugin.options.defaultContent).hide();
    $this.find(plugin.options.hoverContent).show();
  }
  else if(activeEvent === "mouseleave"){
  }
}
```

15. If the `activeEvent` variable is `mouseleave`, we will first hide the hover content using the `jQuery.hide()` method and then show the default content using the `jQuery.show()` method. This is done as follows:

```
action: function(e){
  var plugin = $(e.delegateTarget).data("plugin_" + pluginName),
  activeEvent = e.type,
  $this = $(this);

  if(activeEvent === "mouseenter"){
    $this.find(plugin.options.defaultContent).hide();
    $this.find(plugin.options.hoverContent).show();
  }
  else if(activeEvent === "mouseleave"){
    $this.find(plugin.options.defaultContent).show();
    $this.find(plugin.options.hoverContent).hide();
  }
}
```

16. So that's our action event done. Now, the final thing is to fire our plugin in the `main.js` file using `$('.hoverpanels').hoverpanels()`, which is done as follows:

```
(function(){
  $('.hoverpanels').hoverpanels();
}());
```

Now if we test this on our browser, we should be able to hover over the panels and the content should swap out, allowing you to see the hover content instead of the default content.

Writing a carousel with jQuery Boilerplate (Intermediate)

Carousels are very common across many websites, and being a web developer, it is essential you know how to code one.

Getting Ready

Before you get started with your carousel, you will need to find yourself five images of the same size to be your carousel content. These can be anything, from simple images numbered 1 to 5 (as I will be using) to photos of friends or family.

We will once again use the template that we previously set up.

How to do it...

1. We will start by setting up the HTML for our carousel. This will simply consist of an unordered list within a carousel `div` wrapper. Each of the list items is populated with the images that you have selected to use inside your carousel:

```
<div class="carousel">
  <ul>
    <li><img src="images/item1.jpg" alt="" /></li>
    <li><img src="images/item2.jpg" alt="" /></li>
    <li><img src="images/item3.jpg" alt="" /></li>
    <li><img src="images/item4.jpg" alt="" /></li>
    <li><img src="images/item5.jpg" alt="" /></li>
  </ul>
</div>
```

2. Users without JavaScript will simply get a list of the images. Now for users with JavaScript, we are going to add the carousel's functionality to our list.

3. The first thing we need to do is name our plugin. There are lots of plugins, so simply calling it a carousel will cause issues; so for this example, we will call our plugin `boilerplatecarousel`. We will need to update the `pluginName` variable to reflect this as follows:

```
var pluginName = "boilerplatecarousel",
```

4. Our next step is to look at our plugin's `init` method:

    1. To start with, we want to cache our element as `$element`; we do this by setting the `$element` variable equal to `$(this.element)`.

    2. We then need to determine the width of the items and how many items we will be sliding between; the width will be achieved by using `$element.find('li').width()`, and the number of items will be counted using `$element.find('li').length`.

    3. We will then store the jQuery object for the carousel slider in `this.carousel`, and then add a `width` parameter equal to the item width multiplied by the number of items.

    4. We then need to add a controller to allow the user to interact with the carousel; this should include a `next` and `previous` button.

    5. Finally, we need to add a functionality to the buttons that we will use for the event delegation to fire the `this.controller` method:

```
init: function() {
  var $element = $(this.element);

  var $items = $element.find('li');
  var width = $items.width();
  var count = $items.length;

  this.carousel = $element.find('ul');

  this.carousel.css('width',width*count);

  $element.append('<ul class="controller"><li><a
href="#" class="prev">prev</a></li><li><a href="#"
class="next">next</a></li></ul>');

  $element.on('click', '.controller li a', this.
controller);

}
```

5. Once we have set up our `init` function, we need to add some functionality to our `controller` method. As we are sharing one method between both the `next` and `previous` buttons, we will need to identify which button has been clicked on in this method so that we know what the user wants to do. Before we can identify the button that has been clicked on, we need to set up some variables. First we will cache `$(this)` as `$this`, then we will read the `class` parameter of the button that has been clicked and store it as `navClass`, retrieve the plugin instance as `plugin`, and work out which item is currently visible to the user and cache it as `currentItem`. All this is shown in the following code snippet:

```
controller: function(e){
  var $this = $(this),
  navClass = $this.attr('class'),
  plugin = $(e.delegateTarget).data("plugin_" + pluginName),
  $currentItem = $(plugin.element).find('li').first();

  if(navClass.indexOf('next') !== -1){
    $currentItem.appendTo(plugin.carousel);
  }
  else if(navClass.indexOf('prev') !== -1){

    $(plugin.carousel).prepend($(plugin.carousel).find('li').
last());
  }

  return false;
}
```

6. At this point, we currently have the plugin reordering our items; however, it doesn't appear to look much like a carousel as all the items are still visible. To make it appear more like a carousel, we need to look at adding some styles.

7. The first step is to define the styles for our container, which will provide a width for the view area of the carousel and will hide all those items not in the view area. We will define a width of `500px` and use `overflow:hidden` to hide those that are outside of the view area.

```
.carousel{
  overflow: hidden;
  width: 500px;
  position: relative;
}
```

8. We then need to look at the styles of the slider. The `UL` tag itself will need to override the default padding on a `UL` tag by setting `padding: 0px`, and we will use `overflow:hidden` to clear the floats of the items inside the `UL` tag.

```
.carousel ul{
   padding: 0px;
   overflow: hidden;
}
```

9. We will need to style the appearance of the individual items in the carousel. We need all of them to be floated in line with each other, have a width of `500px` to match the view area. Additionally, we need to override the default `list-style` parameter and set its value to `none`. This is done as follows:

```
.carousel ul li{
   float: left;
   width: 500px;
   list-style: none;
}
```

10. Finally, we need to add some styling to both the arrows, which will be achieved by positioning them at the top of the carousel.

```
.carousel ul.controller li a.next,.carousel ul.controller li
a.prev{
   position: absolute;
   top: 140px;
   background: #fff;
   padding: 20px;
}

.carousel ul.controller li a.prev{
   left: 0px;
   border-radius: 0 10px 10px 0;
}

.carousel ul.controller li a.next{
   right: 0px;
   border-radius: 10px 0 0 10px;
}
```

There's more...

At this point, all our carousel is doing is reordering the elements; it is not doing any animation, as one would normally expect in a carousel. We will now add one animation; hopefully, with what you will learn here, you could go on to add your own effects:

1. When working on this extension to the carousel, we are extending our existing carousel plugin.

2. Our first step is to extend the `defaults` object literal to have an extra value for the effect; this will enable the plugin to support multiple effects if you wish.

```
defaults = {
  effect: "none"
};
```

3. We then need to add a new method to our `Plugin` prototype's object literal to handle the effect; we will name this as `effect`.

4. Our first step is to move our existing transition with no effect to the `effect` method, and for this, we will need to write the first part of our `effect` method. To begin with, we will move the `if` statement we previously had in our `controller` method to the `effect` method.

```
effect: function($currentItem, direction){
  if(direction === "next"){
    $currentItem.appendTo(this.carousel);
  }
  else if(direction === "prev"){
    $(this.carousel).prepend($(this.carousel).find('li').last());
  }
}
```

5. We then need to make some changes to our `controller` method so that it uses the new `effect` method for the transition. Where we previously had an `if` statement for the transition, we now have an `if` statement that will fire the `effect` method with the correct parameters, shown as follows:

```
controller: function(e){
  var $this = $(this),
  navClass = $this.attr('class'),
  plugin = $(e.delegateTarget).data("plugin_" +
    pluginName),
  $currentItem = $(plugin.element).find('li').first();
```

```
  if(navClass.indexOf('next') !== -1){
    plugin.effect($currentItem, "next");
  }
  else if(navClass.indexOf('prev') !== -1){
    plugin.effect($currentItem, "prev");
  }

  return false;
}
```

6. At this point, our carousel should work in the same way as before, cycling through each of the items in the carousel one-by-one with no animation. Now, we can extend our `effects` method to provide extra transitions. The first step is to create an `if` statement that selects which `effect` should be used. The idea is that, if the developer using the plugin has not indicated which effect they want, it will resort to the default `no` effect.

```
effect: function($currentItem, direction){
  var itemWidth = $currentItem.width();

  if(this.options.effect === "slide"){
    //slide effect will go here
  }
  else if(this.options.effect === "none"){
    if(direction === "next"){
      $currentItem.appendTo(this.carousel);
    }
    else if(direction === "prev"){
      $(this.carousel).prepend($(this.carousel).find('li').
last());
    }
  }
}
```

7. Once we are happy with our `if` statement, we can start working on our slide effect. For the effect to work, we need to animate the sliding of the UL containing the carousel's items to the left and right. The view area of the carousel is only set to the width of one item, so moving the UL tag within this will show our desired animation.

8. As per the `no` animation effect, we first need to add a simple `if` statement that reads the `direction` parameter of the `effect` method and allows us to handle both directions.

```
effect: function($currentItem, direction){
  var itemWidth = $currentItem.width();
```

```
    if(this.options.effect === "slide"){
      if(direction === "next"){
      }
      else if(direction === "prev"){
      }
    }
    else if(this.options.effect === "none"){
      if(direction === "next"){
        $currentItem.appendTo(this.carousel);
      }
      else if(direction === "prev"){
        $(this.carousel).prepend($(this.carousel).find('li').
          last());
      }
    }
  }
}
```

9. Once we have the `if` statement, we are able to start working on our logic inside it. Our first step is to work on the code required for when our first condition is met, which is when the `direction` variable is equal to `next`.

10. For this, we are going to use the `jQuery.animate()` function to animate the shifting of the `UL` containing the items on the left. The distance travelled will equal the width of one of the carousel items. As the complete function parameter, we move the item to the end of the list of items and then reset the `left` value to `0px`.

```
effect: function($currentItem, direction){
  var itemWidth = $currentItem.width();

  if(this.options.effect === "slide"){
    if(direction === "next"){
      $(this.carousel).animate({
        left: "-="+itemWidth
      }, 500, function() {
          $(this).find('li').first().appendTo(this);
          $(this).css('left','0px');
        });
    }
    else if(direction === "prev"){

    }
  }
  else if(this.options.effect === "none"){
    if(direction === "next"){
      $currentItem.appendTo(this.carousel);
    }
```

```
     else if(direction === "prev"){
       $(this.carousel).prepend($(this.carousel).find('li').
         last());
     }
   }
 }
```

11. Moving to the previous `direction` is not as simple. Firstly, we need to move the last carousel item to the beginning of the `UL` tag containing the items; then we need to set the position of the `UL` so that the current item is still visible. Finally, we need to use the `jQuery.animate()` function to move to the previous item. The main problem with this is that this function does not allow us to provide it with functionality before the animation. Along with this, we need to ensure that, if the user clicks on the previous button *X* times, then we need to move an *X* number of items. This means we need to look at how we can manipulate the animation queue. jQuery provides us with a way to do this using `.queue()`. In its simplest form, we only need to provide one parameter, which is our method that we wish to queue. This will add the method to be called as part of the `fx` queue.

```
effect: function($currentItem, direction){
  var itemWidth = $currentItem.width();

  if(this.options.effect === "slide"){
    if(direction === "next"){
      $(this.carousel).animate({
        left: "-="+itemWidth
      }, 500, function() {
        $(this).find('li').first().appendTo(this);
        $(this).css('left','0px');
      });
    }
    else if(direction === "prev"){
      $(this.carousel).queue(function () { });
    }
  }
  else if(this.options.effect === "none"){
    if(direction === "next"){
      $currentItem.appendTo(this.carousel);
    }
    else if(direction === "prev"){
      $(this.carousel).prepend($(this.carousel).find('li').
        last());
    }
  }
}
```

12. Now when we click on the previous button, we will be adding a new item to the `fx` queue. Next, though, we need to add the functionality that we previously discussed to the queue. (Rather than repeating the code, we will now only show the queue). The first thing we need to do is create a variable in which we will store the queue; we will call this `currentQueue` and will set the value to `null`. We then need to move the last item to the beginning of the list and set the left position of the `UL` item list to be `0` minus the width of 1 item.

```
$(this.carousel).queue(function () {
   var currentQueue = null;

   $(this).prepend($(this).find('li').last());
   $(this).css('left',-itemWidth);
});
```

13. We can then look at adding our animation. We do this in the same way we used the `jQuery.animate()` function previously; however, this time we are moving the `UL` item container in a positive direction. We will also not find the need to pass a callback method as, once the animation is complete, the items will be in the correct place. The code snippet to do this is as follows:

```
$(this.carousel).queue(function () {
   var currentQueue = null,
   var $this = $(this);

   $this.prepend($(this).find('li').last());
   $this.css('left',-itemWidth);

   $this.animate({
      left: "+="+itemWidth
   }, 500)
});
```

14. We have added our animation to the queue using `.animate()`; however, this will add it to the end of the queue; if the user has clicked on the button multiple times, the animation will be a bit strange. Thus, we now need to re-sort the order of the `fx` queue so that it flows correctly. To start with, we will now use the `currentQueue` variable we declared earlier to store our queue, which can be retrieved using `$(this).queue()`. We then need to move the last item of the array to be the second item in the array (so that it is fired next). We do this by using `.splice()` with the index of 1, howMany set to 0 (so that we do not remove any items) and we pass the last element of the array as the value to add into the array. We can then simply use `.pop()` to remove the last item from the queue as we have already moved it to the new position. We then need to update the `fx` queue array with the values of the updated queue that we have manipulated.

```
$(this.carousel).queue(function () {
   var currentQueue = $(this).queue(),
```

```
  var $this = $(this);

  $this.prepend($(this).find('li').last());
  $this.css('left',-itemWidth);

  $this.animate({
    left: "+="+itemWidth
  }, 500);

  currentQueue = $(this).queue();

  currentQueue.splice(1, 0, currentQueue[currentQueue.length-1]);
  currentQueue.pop();

  $(this).queue(currentQueue);
});
```

15. Finally we need to add $(this).dequeue() at the end of the method, which will then remove this function from the queue and trigger the next item to be fired. As we just made our next item to be animation, our animation item will now trigger.

```
$(this.carousel).queue(function () {
  var currentQueue = null;

  $(this).prepend($(this).find('li').last());
  $(this).css('left',-itemWidth);

  $(this).animate({
    left: "+="+itemWidth
  }, 500);

  currentQueue = $(this).queue();

  currentQueue.splice(1, 0,
    currentQueue[currentQueue.length-1]);
  currentQueue.pop();

  $(this).queue(currentQueue);

  $(this).dequeue();
});
```

16. Now that we have finished this, our previous button should work, so try clicking on it. You should find that you're able to click on it multiple times with the animation remaining smooth.

AJAX bookshelves with jQuery Boilerplate (Advanced)

Previous plugins have been about manipulating existing content. For more advanced readers, we will now look at how we can use AJAX to retrieve a list of books that the site owner has been reading.

It will pull this list of books into the plugin and build a pull-out sidebar on the website that will list all the books and provide different ways in which they can be sorted.

Getting ready

For this recipe, we will use a copy of the template we created in the previous recipe.

Using our base template from the previous recipe, we will start out by creating a new file called `data.json` in the root of the project; this will house the list of our books as JSON. For each book we will store the ISBN, Name, Author, Publisher, and an image.

```
[
  {
    "isbn": "1849516529",
    "name": "jQuery UI 1.8: The User Interface Library for
      jQuery",
    "author": "Dan Wellman",
    "publisher": "PACKT Publishing",
    "cover": "images/6525OS_jQuery UI 1.8_Front cover_0.jpg"
  },
  {
    "isbn": "9781849510042",
    "name": "jQuery 1.4 Reference Guide",
    "author": "Jonathan Chaffer, Karl Swedberg",
    "publisher": "PACKT Publishing",
    "cover": "images/0042_MockupCover_0.jpg"
  },
  {
    "isbn": "1849516545",
    "name": "Learning jQuery, Third Edition",
    "author": "Jonathan Chaffer, Karl Swedberg",
    "publisher": "PACKT Publishing",
    "cover": "images/6549OS_Learning jQuery Third
      Edition_FrontCover.jpg"
  }
]
```

How to do it...

1. To ensure that your JSON does not contain any errors, I recommend you **lint** the JSON using **JSON Lint** (`http://jsonlint.com/`). This will enable you to ensure you have not made any mistakes with the syntax of your JSON.

2. The next step after you have got your JSON is for us to start writing our plugin; as we are using our template, we can simply open `plugin.js` to get started. As with our other plugins, the first step when writing our plugin is to name it; in this case we will name it `bookshelf`.

   ```
   var pluginName = "bookshelf",
   ```

3. Following on from this, we need to set our defaults. We want our user to be able to configure both the URL of the book's data file, and the name of the bookshelf they are adding to their site. We will name these options `url` with a default value of `null` and `bookshelfName` with a default value of `My Bookshelf`.

   ```
   var pluginName = "bookshelf",
   defaults = {
     url : null,
     bookshelfName: "My Bookshelf"
   };
   ```

4. We also have an extra variable to add to the top of our plugin called `templates`, which will store an object literal of templates that will be used by the plugin for generating the HTML for the bookshelf. The `templates` object will contain two templates, the first being the main bookshelf container, and the second the template used for each book added to the bookshelf. To allow our templates to be flexible for us to add content to, we will use placeholder text, starting and ending with the `%` symbols so that we can replace these with the actual text when we are generating our HTML.

   ```
   var templates = {
     container    : "<div
       id='bookshelf'><h1>%BookshelfName%</h1><a class='pull'
         href='#'>Pull</a><div
           id='bookshelf_books'></div></div>",
     book: "<div class='book'><h2>%Title%</h2><img
       src='%Cover%'/><p>%Author%</p><p>%Publisher%</p></div>"
   };
   ```

5. As our plugin is only ever going to have one instance and it needs to exist on the body of the page, we will now make some tweaks to the plugin wrapper. The key change is that, rather than looping through items passed to the plugin, we are simply checking for a current instance of the plugin on the body. If none is found, we create a new instance of the plugin on the body and then simply return `this`.

```
$.fn[pluginName] = function ( options ) {

  if (!$.data(document.body, "plugin_" + pluginName)) {
    $.data(document.body, "plugin_" + pluginName, new
      Plugin(document.body, options ));
  }

  return this;
};
```

6. This change also has implications on how we call our plugin from our `main.js` file; regardless of whether a selector is passed to jQuery or not, the plugin will always apply itself to the body. The benefit of this is that now we can simply use `$().bookshelf({url: "data.json"})` to set up our plugin. We should now update this in the `main.js` file.

7. Our next step is to make a start on our `init` method. Begin by checking that the developer using our plugin has provided a URL for the book feed to the plugin. To do this we will simply check to see `this.options.url` does not equal `null`. In the event that the URL has not been provided, we will then determine whether the browser console is available and if so, we will output an error to notify the developer they haven't passed a URL to the plugin. Finally we will use `return false` to exit out of the `init` method without executing the rest of the method.

```
init: function() {
  if(this.options.url === null){
    //cannot do anything without a URL

    return false;
  }
},
```

8. If we want to test whether this works, we can simply change our call to the plugin in the `main.js` file to not pass any parameters so the code will look like `$().bookshelf()`. We can then open the page in our browser and, upon opening the browser console, we will see that our plugin has an output similar to the error message shown in the following screenshot:

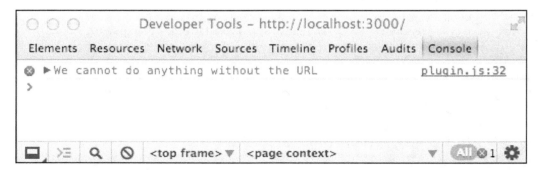

9. Having tested that our check for the URL works correctly, we can change the call to the plugin in the `main.js` file back to `$().bookshelf({url: "data.json"})`.

10. Now that we are sure that the developer using our plugin has provided the URL to the data feed, we are able to continue to initialize our plugin. We will need to add the `bookshelf` container to the page, which can be achieved by using simple JavaScript to add to the `innerHTML` of the body element. At the point of adding the bookshelf container to the page, we also need to update the bookshelf name. This can be achieved by using `.replace()` to replace `%BookshelfName%` with `this.options.bookshelfName`. To keep this simple, we can perform the replace action on the template and append it directly to the body HTML. The init function can be written as follows for this purpose:

```
init: function() {

  //make sure the user defines a URL for the plugin or else
  //log an error to the console
  if(this.options.url === null){
    if(typeof console !== "undefined") {
      console.error('We cannot do anything without the
        URL');
    }

    return false;
  }

  //setup empty bookshelf
  this.element.innerHTML +=
    templates.container.replace('%BookshelfName%',
      this.options.bookshelfName);
},
```

11. It is at this point that we can do our book lookup; as the page already has the bookshelf loaded, it is ready for us to get our JSON feed using AJAX. We will do this by using the `jQuery.getJSON()` method combined with the `jQuery.proxy()` method, which we are using to allow us to maintain the correct scope of this in our `this.outputBooks` method:

```
init: function() {

  if(this.options.url === null){
    //cannot do anything without a URL
    if(typeof console !== "undefined") {
      console.error('We cannot do anything without the
        URL');
    }
  }
```

```
      return false;
    }

    //setup empty bookshelf
    this.element.innerHTML +=
      templates.container.replace('%BookshelfName%',
        this.options.bookshelfName);

    //Get books
    $.getJSON(this.options.url, $.proxy(this.outputBooks, this));
  },
```

12. Our final step in our `init` method is for us to add the click functionality to our toggle button that shows and hides our bookshelf. We will add this as an event delegated from the `body` element and clicking on the button will call the `this.toggleVisible` method that we will be creating shortly:

```
init: function() {

  $(this.element).on('click', '#bookshelf .pull',
    this.toggleVisible);
},
```

13. As you have seen in our `init` method, we will need to add a couple of extra methods to our `Plugin` prototype. The first of these is `outputBooks`, the second `toggleVisible`, so we will now take a moment to add these methods as follows:

```
Plugin.prototype = {
  init: function() {

    if(this.options.url === null){
      //cannot do anything without a URL
      if(typeof console !== "undefined") {
        console.error('We cannot do anything without the
          URL');
      }

      return false;
    }

    //setup empty bookshelf
    this.element.innerHTML +=
      templates.container.replace('%BookshelfName%',
        this.options.bookshelfName);
```

```
//Get books
$.getJSON(this.options.url, $.proxy(this.outputBooks,
    this));

$(this.element).on('click', '#bookshelf .pull',
    this.toggleVisible);
},
outputBooks: function(data){

},
toggleVisible: function(){

}
};
```

14. With these in place we are ready to start handling the output of our books to our bookshelf. This is handled by our `outputBooks` method. The first step for our `outputBooks` method is for us to set up our variables. We need to append to the bookshelf container so we will retrieve the element using `document.getElementById`. The reason to use native JavaScript rather than jQuery to select the element is that we will not be requiring any jQuery functionality; thus, for slightly better performance, we will choose to use native JavaScript. We also need two variables to cache generated HTML before it is added to the book container; these are `booksHTML` and `bookHTML`:

```
outputBooks: function(data){
    var bookshelfBooks = document.getElementById('bookshelf_books'),
        booksHTML = "",
        bookHTML = "";
},
```

15. Now that our variables are set up, we can start looking at the data that was returned by the `jQuery.getJSON()` method. The method has passed the data as the first parameter of our method that we have named `data`. The data is made up of an array of books so we will use a `for` loop to loop through the books stored in the `data` array so that we can process them one by one.

```
outputBooks: function(data){
    var bookshelfBooks =
        document.getElementById('bookshelf_books'),
    booksHTML = "",
    bookHTML = "";

    for (var i = 0; i < data.length; i++) {
    }
},
```

16. As part of our loop we need to first retrieve the template for a book from the template object this will be stored in the `bookHTML` variable. We will then use `.replace()` to start updating the templated HTML with the correct values from the current data item. This will need to be done for the title, author, publisher, and cover.

```
outputBooks: function(data){
  var bookshelfBooks =
    document.getElementById('bookshelf_books'),
  booksHTML = "",
  bookHTML = "";

  for (var i = 0; i < data.length; i++) {
    //Setup book with default template
    bookHTML = templates.book;

    //Fill in the template
    bookHTML = bookHTML.replace("%Title%",data[i].name);
    bookHTML = bookHTML.replace("%Author%",data[i].author);
    bookHTML = bookHTML.replace("%Publisher%",data[i].publisher);
    bookHTML = bookHTML.replace("%Cover%",data[i].cover);
  }
},
```

17. After we have built up the HTML for our individual books, we now need to add it to our `booksHTML` variable that is used to contain the details of all the books we have just retrieved:

```
outputBooks: function(data){
  var bookshelfBooks =
    document.getElementById('bookshelf_books'),
  booksHTML = "",
  bookHTML = "";

  for (var i = 0; i < data.length; i++) {
    //Setup book with default template
    bookHTML = templates.book;
```

```
    //Fill in the template
    bookHTML = bookHTML.replace("%Title%",data[i].name);
    bookHTML = bookHTML.replace("%Author%",data[i].author);
    bookHTML =
      bookHTML.replace("%Publisher%",data[i].publisher);
    bookHTML = bookHTML.replace("%Cover%",data[i].cover);

    booksHTML += bookHTML;
  }
},
```

18. After our loop has built up the HTML for all our books, we now need to append it to the `bookshelf` container. We will append it by simply adding to the `innerHTML` variable of the container. The code snippet for this purpose is as follows:

```
outputBooks: function(data){
  var bookshelfBooks =
    document.getElementById('bookshelf_books'),
  booksHTML = "",
  bookHTML = "";

  for (var i = 0; i < data.length; i++) {
    //Setup book with default template
    bookHTML = templates.book;

    //Fill in the template
    bookHTML = bookHTML.replace("%Title%",data[i].name);
    bookHTML = bookHTML.replace("%Author%",data[i].author);
    bookHTML =
      bookHTML.replace("%Publisher%",data[i].publisher);
    bookHTML = bookHTML.replace("%Cover%",data[i].cover);

    booksHTML += bookHTML;
  }

  bookshelfBooks.innerHTML += booksHTML;
},
```

19. At this point, our plugin should be able to render the information about our books to the page; however, without any proper styling it simply shows as a list of books. Our aim is to style it to be a pull-out bookshelf anchored to the right of the page:

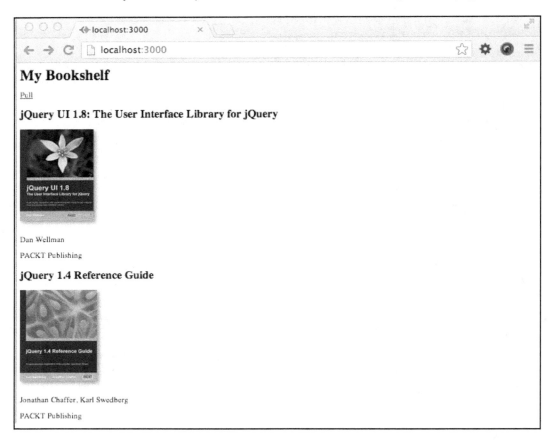

20. At this point we will take a break from working on the JavaScript for our plugin so that we can add the necessary styling to enable us to add the pull-out functionality. Next we need to position our bookshelf. We want this to be fixed to the side of the browser viewport. This will be achieved simply by using `position: fixed`, `top: 0px` and `right: -200px`, the reason we set the right to a negative value is that it appears off the edge of the screen to begin with. We will also set the background color to a wood color and set the height to `100%` so that it fills the browser's viewport height:

```
#bookshelf{
  position: fixed;
  background : #e9c2a6;
  top: 0px;
  right: -200px;
  width: 200px;
  height: 100%;
}
```

21. The next step is to allow the wrapper for the books to show a scrollbar if the books overflow outside of the wrapper. This can be done in the following way:

```
#bookshelf #bookshelf_books{
  overflow: auto;
  position: absolute;
  top: 50px;
  left: 0px;
  bottom: 0px;
  width: 200px;
}
```

22. We now want to style our title. The code for this can be written as follows:

```
#bookshelf h1{
  font-size: 1.6em;
  padding: 10px 20px;
  margin: 0px;
  border-bottom: 3px solid #000;
  line-height: 27px;
  background : #e9c2a6;
  z-index: 99;
  position: relative;
}
```

23. We will style the individual book items so that there is spacing around each book and a border at the bottom dividing the books, as shown in the following code snippet:

```
#bookshelf .book{
  padding: 10px 20px;
  border-bottom: 1px solid #000;
}
```

24. We also want to ensure that the image for our book does not extend beyond the width of the book item, so we will set a `width` variable in our CSS as follows:

```
#bookshelf .book img{
   width: 160px;
}
```

25. Finally, we will add the styling for the `pull` tab that we will use to toggle in order to know whether our bookshelf is open or closed, as shown:

```
#bookshelf .pull{
   position: absolute;
   left: -50px;
   top: 50%;
   line-height: 40px;
   margin-top: -20px;
   background : #e9c2a6;
   width: 50px;
   text-align: center;
   text-decoration: none;
}
```

26. With our styling complete, we will now see only a tab when we load the page as shown in the following screenshot. However, without our JavaScript, at the moment it will not do anything; we will be unable to see the bookshelf until we write our `toggleVisible` method:

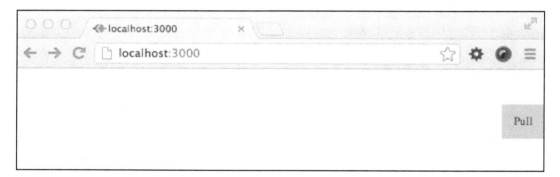

27. Moving on to the `pull` tab functionality, we need to work on our `toggleVisible` method. Our first step is to set up our variables. For this we will simply store the jQuery object for `this` as `$this`.

```
toggleVisible: function(){
   var $this = $(this);
}
```

28. We are going to manage the state of the `pull` tab by toggling the `active` class; therefore, our next step is to check whether `$this` has the `active` class or not. We check using the `if` statement as follows:

```
toggleVisible: function(){
  var $this = $(this);

  if($this.hasClass('active')){
  }
  else{
  }
}
```

29. With our `if` statement in place we now want to animate the bookshelf so that when it is not active it slides open, and when it is already active it slides closed. To perform the animation we will use `jQuery.animate()` applied directly to the bookshelf container; we will also use `.stop()` to stop any existing animation. The code snippet to achieve this is as follows:

```
toggleVisible: function(){
  var $this = $(this);

  if($this.hasClass('active')){
    $('#bookshelf').stop().animate({
      right: '-200px'
    }, 250);
  }
  else{
    $('#bookshelf').stop().animate({
      right: '0px'
    }, 250);
  }
}
```

30. Our next step is to toggle our `active` class. The code snippet for toggling it is as follows:

```
toggleVisible: function(){
  var $this = $(this);

  if($this.hasClass('active')){
    $('#bookshelf').stop().animate({
      right: '-200px'
    }, 250);
  }
```

```
    else{
      $('#bookshelf').stop().animate({
        right: '0px'
      }, 250);
    }

    $this.toggleClass('active');
  }
```

31. Our final step is to add `return false` at the end of the method so that the default action of the `anchor` tag used for the `pull` tab is not executed.

```
  toggleVisible: function(){
    var $this = $(this);

    if($this.hasClass('active')){
      $('#bookshelf').stop().animate({
        right: '-200px'
      }, 250);
    }
    else{
      $('#bookshelf').stop().animate({
        right: '0px'
      }, 250);
    }

    $this.toggleClass('active');

    return false;
  }
```

32. At this point our plugin should work; the pull tab should be clickable and it should toggle the visibility of the bookshelf.

There's more...

Now that we have completed our base plugin, we can think about ways in which we can extend it.

Extending our plugin

There are many ways in which we can extend our plugin. A couple of ideas are that we can add support to detect whether we should use normal JSON or JSONP, or allow the site visitors to bookmark their favorite books.

As the second option is quite interesting, because it allows us to explore and use the HTML5 `localStorage` API to cache user preferences, we will be choosing and following this option.

The first step when extending our plugin is to create a copy of what we have done; this will allow us to go back to the old version if we want. Alternatively, we could use source control to manage this plugin.

1. Once we are ready, we first need to start making changes to the JavaScript plugin. We need to amend the `book` template to add a link to toggle whether the book is a favorite or not. To correctly identify the book, we will use the ISBN as a unique identifier that we will store in the `href` tag of the link. The code snippet for this is as follows:

```
var templates = {
   container    : "<div id='bookshelf'><h1>%BookshelfName%</h1><a
      class='pull' href='#'>Pull</a><div
        id='bookshelf_books'></div></div>",
   book: "<div class='book'><h2>%Title%</h2><img
      src='%Cover%'/><p>%Author%</p><p>%Publisher%</p><p><a
        class='fav_link' href='#%ISBN%'>%Favourite%</a></p></div>"
};
```

2. We also want to enable the developers who are using our plugin to be able to customize the text that is shown on the **Add to/Remove from Favorites** button so we will add two new `default` options to the `defaults` object. The first is `favAddText` and the second `favRemoveText`. The code snippet for this is as follows:

```
var pluginName = "bookshelf",
   defaults = {
     url : null,
     bookshelfName: "My Bookshelf",
     favAddText: "Add to favourites",
     favRemoveText: "Remove from favourites"
   };
```

3. Once we have updated our template and default values, we need to amend our `outputBooks` method. To start with, our `outputBooks` method should already look like the following:

```
outputBooks: function(data){
   var bookshelfBooks = document.getElementById('bookshelf_books'),
   booksHTML = "",
   bookHTML = "";
```

```
      for (var i = 0; i < data.length; i++) {
        //Setup book with default template
        bookHTML = templates.book;

        //Fill in the template
        bookHTML = bookHTML.replace("%Title%",data[i].name);
        bookHTML = bookHTML.replace("%Author%",data[i].author);
        bookHTML = bookHTML.replace("%Publisher%",data[i].publisher);
        bookHTML = bookHTML.replace("%Cover%",data[i].cover);

        booksHTML += bookHTML;
      }

      bookshelfBooks.innerHTML += booksHTML;
    },
```

4. The first thing we need to add to the method is the population of the ISBN number; to do this we will simply add another `replace` method to the `bookHTML` variable to update the ISBN. The code snippet for this is as follows:

```
outputBooks: function(data){
    var bookshelfBooks =
      document.getElementById('bookshelf_books'),
    booksHTML = "",
    bookHTML = "";

    for (var i = 0; i < data.length; i++) {
      //Setup book with default template
      bookHTML = templates.book;

      //Fill in the template
      bookHTML = bookHTML.replace("%Title%",data[i].name);
      bookHTML = bookHTML.replace("%Author%",data[i].author);
      bookHTML =
        bookHTML.replace("%Publisher%",data[i].publisher);
      bookHTML = bookHTML.replace("%Cover%",data[i].cover);
      bookHTML = bookHTML.replace("%ISBN%",data[i].isbn);
      bookHTML = bookHTML.replace("%ISBN%",data[i].isbn);
      booksHTML += bookHTML;
    }

    bookshelfBooks.innerHTML += booksHTML;
  },
```

5. We now need to determine whether the current book has been stored as a favorite. To manage favorites, we will be storing the ISBN in local storage with the book's ISBN as the key and the value being `true`. When an item is removed from being a favorite, the item in local storage will also be removed. To check if a book is a favorite, we simply need to verify if a local storage item exists for that particular ISBN. If an item does not exist, `localStorage.getItem` will simply return `null`. Therefore, we will add an `if` statement that checks if it returns `null`. The code snippet for this is as follows:

```
outputBooks: function(data){
  var bookshelfBooks = document.getElementById('bookshelf_books'),
  booksHTML = "",
  bookHTML = "";

  for (var i = 0; i < data.length; i++) {
    //Setup book with default template
    bookHTML = templates.book;

    //Fill in the template
    bookHTML = bookHTML.replace("%Title%",data[i].name);
    bookHTML = bookHTML.replace("%Author%",data[i].author);
    bookHTML = bookHTML.replace("%Publisher%",data[i].publisher);
    bookHTML = bookHTML.replace("%Cover%",data[i].cover);
    bookHTML = bookHTML.replace("%ISBN%",data[i].isbn);

    if(localStorage.getItem(data[i].isbn) !== null){
    }
    else{
    }

    booksHTML += bookHTML;
  }

  bookshelfBooks.innerHTML += booksHTML;
},
```

6. With our `if` statement in place, we can now update the `favorite` link with the correct copy, and if a book is a favorite, we will add an extra class to the book to which we can add our favorite book styles:

```
outputBooks: function(data){
  var bookshelfBooks =
    document.getElementById('bookshelf_books'),
  booksHTML = "",
  bookHTML = "";
```

```
        for (var i = 0; i < data.length; i++) {
          //Setup book with default template
          bookHTML = templates.book;

          //Fill in the template
          bookHTML = bookHTML.replace("%Title%",data[i].name);
          bookHTML =
            bookHTML.replace("%Author%",data[i].author);
          bookHTML =
            bookHTML.replace("%Publisher%",data[i].publisher);
          bookHTML = bookHTML.replace("%Cover%",data[i].cover);
          bookHTML = bookHTML.replace("%ISBN%",data[i].isbn);

          if(localStorage.getItem(data[i].isbn) !== null){
            bookHTML =
              bookHTML.replace("class='book'","class='book
                fav'");
            bookHTML =
              bookHTML.replace("%Favourite%",this.options.
                favRemoveText);
          }
          else{
            bookHTML =
              bookHTML.replace("%Favourite%",this.options.favAddText);
          }

          booksHTML += bookHTML;
        }

      bookshelfBooks.innerHTML += booksHTML;
    },
```

7. At this stage we can test out the plugin in our browser. You should see that each book now has a new link called **Add to favorites**. At this time we haven't added the functionality to actually add the book to become a favorite, so clicking on the links will not perform any action.

8. We now need to look at the functionality for our favorite links, the first step of which is to add the `toggleFavourite` method to our `Plugin.prototype` object. We will be using the jQuery event object to get the current instance of the plugin so this is passed to our method as `e`, as shown:

```
toggleFavourite: function(e){
}
```

9. We will then define our variables. For this method we will need $this, the plugin instance as plugin, the selected book as $book, and isbn that is the ISBN number of the book, which we will retrieve from the href of the button clicked:

```
toggleFavourite: function(e){
  var $this = $(this),
  plugin = $(e.delegateTarget).data("plugin_" +
    pluginName),
  $book = $this.parents('.book'),
  isbn = $this.attr('href').replace('#','');
}
```

10. We now need to determine whether the button that has been clicked needs to add or remove a favorite. We will do this by attempting to get the item from the local storage using the isbn as the key. If the result is null, we know that we are adding a favorite; otherwise we want to remove a favorite:

```
toggleFavourite: function(e){
  var $this = $(this),
  plugin = $(e.delegateTarget).data("plugin_" +
    pluginName),
  $book = $this.parents('.book'),
  isbn = $this.attr('href').replace('#','');

  if(localStorage.getItem(isbn) === null){
  }
  else{
  }

  return false;
}
```

11. With our if statement in place we can now add the functionality. To add a favorite we want to create a new item in the local storage using localStorage.setItem. We then want to add a class to the book element to denote that this particular book is in our favorites and allow us to apply styles to show it is a favorite. We also want to change the text of the favorite link so that it reads Remove from favorites, which we will retrieve from our plugin options. This is shown in the following code snippet:

```
toggleFavourite: function(e){
  var $this = $(this),
  plugin = $(e.delegateTarget).data("plugin_" +
    pluginName),
  $book = $this.parents('.book'),
  isbn = $this.attr('href').replace('#','');
```

```
if(localStorage.getItem(isbn) === null){
  localStorage.setItem(isbn, true);
  $book.addClass('fav');
    $this.html(plugin.options.favRemoveText);
}
else{
}

return false;
}
```

12. In the `else` part of the `if` statement, we want to remove the item from favorites. To do this we will use `localStorage.remove` to remove the item from the local storage. We will remove the class from the book and then change the text of our favorites link so that it reads `Add to favorites`, which we will retrieve from our plugin options. The code snippet for this is as follows:

```
toggleFavourite: function(e){
  var $this = $(this),
  plugin = $(e.delegateTarget).data("plugin_" + pluginName),
  $book = $this.parents('.book'),
  isbn = $this.attr('href').replace('#','');

  if(localStorage.getItem(isbn) === null){
    localStorage.setItem(isbn, true);
    $book.addClass('fav');
    $this.html(plugin.options.favRemoveText);
  }
  else{
    localStorage.removeItem(isbn);
    $book.removeClass('fav');
    $this.html(plugin.options.favAddText);
  }

  return false;
}
```

13. With our `toggleFavourite` method completed, we can now add an event to the **Add to favorite** link. We will add this to the plugin `init` method. One thing you might notice if you follow through the code is that, when we are in the `init` method, the links have yet to be added to the page. This would be a problem if we were trying to add the event listeners to the individual links; however, we are going to use event delegation so that, instead of adding an event listener to the individual links, we place one event listener on the bookshelf itself:

```
init: function() {

    if(this.options.url === null){
      //cannot do anything without a URL
      if(typeof console !== "undefined") {
        console.error('We cannot do anything without the
          URL');
      }

      return false;
    }

    //setup empty bookshelf
    this.element.innerHTML +=
      templates.container.replace('%BookshelfName%',
        this.options.bookshelfName);

    //Get books
    $.getJSON(this.options.url, $.proxy(this.outputBooks,
        this));

    $(this.element).on('click', '#bookshelf .pull',
      this.toggleVisible);

    $(this.element).on('click', '.book a.fav_link',
      this.toggleFavourite);
},
```

14. At this point if we go back to our browser, we will see that `favorites` are working. For items in our `favorites`, the link text will read **Remove from favorites** and all the other links will read **Add to favorites**. To make it clearer to the user of the site, we will add some simple styles to the `main.css` file to change the background color of the book element to a darker one.

```
#bookshelf .book.fav{
  background: #dfa67d;
}
```

15. With the new CSS in place, the fact that an item is favorited it is clearer to the users of the site. We now have a bookshelf plugin that allows users to mark their favorite books, as shown in the following screenshot:

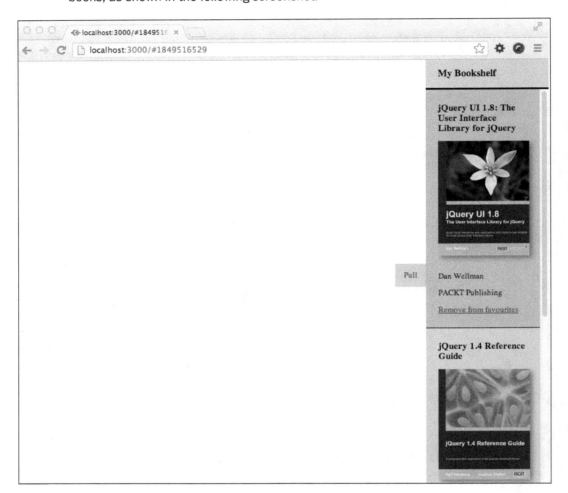

Writing a validation plugin using jQuery Boilerplate (Intermediate)

Basic form validation can be extremely simple to implement with a plugin, but writing a plugin that serves a large number of use cases can be difficult. As such, this section shall show how to build a robust form validation plugin, which validates required e-mail and phone number input fields.

Getting ready

We firstly need our plugin development template created earlier in the book.

How to do it...

1. Our first step is to work on our HTML; for this plugin, we want the JavaScript to require minimal setup once it is pointed to a form, which it needs to validate. To do this, we will need to add data attributes to HTML that define what validation needs to be performed and the error messages that will need to be displayed to the users.

2. The first data attribute we need to add to each of the `input` elements is `data-validate`. This data attribute is used to list all the different validators we want to run against the control. In the following example of an `email` field, we will set `data-validate` to `required email`, which tells JavaScript that we need to validate and check whether an e-mail address has been entered in the field:

   ```
   <input type="text" name="email" data-validate="required
       email"/>
   ```

3. We also want to allow the user of our plugin to customize their error messages; to do this, we will take a similar approach to how we define the validators the element uses. Continuing with the example of an `email` field, we will need to provide error messages for both when the e-mail address has not been filled in and when the e-mail address provided is invalid. To do this, we will add two data attributes: `data-required`, which displays an error message if the e-mail ID is not entered, and `data-email`, which displays an error message if the e-mail ID is not valid:

   ```
   <input type="text" name="email" data-validate="required
       email" data-required="Please tell us your email address"
       data-email="Please enter a valid email address" />
   ```

4. Continuing on, we can now do the same for both a name field and a phone number field. The code snippet for this purpose is as follows:

   ```
   <input type="text" name="name" data-validate="required"
       data-required="Please tell us your name" />
   ```

```
<input type="text" name="email" data-validate="required
  email" data-required="Please tell us your email address"
  data-email="Please enter a valid email address" />

<input type="text" name="phone" data-validate="required
  phone" data-required="Please tell us your phone number"
  data-phone="Please enter a valid phone number" />
```

5. Now that we have the HTML markup for our fields, we can create the rest of the form; this is simply the `form` element wrapping the fields and the addition of a `submit` button. This should be placed in our container in our `index.html` file, as shown in the following code snippet:

```
<form action="#" method="post">
  <label for="name">Name</label>
  <input type="text" name="name" data-validate="required"
    data-required="Please tell us your name" />

  <label for="email">Email</label>
  <input type="text" name="email" data-validate="required
    email" data-required="Please tell us your email
      address" data-email="Please enter a valid email
        address" />

  <label for="phone">Phone number</label>
  <input type="text" name="phone" data-validate="required
      phone" data-required="Please tell us your phone
        number" data-phone="Please enter a valid phone
          number" />

  <input type="submit" value="Submit" />
</form>
```

6. Now that we have our HTML, we can move on to writing our plugin. The first step is to set up our plugin name. For simplicity, we will call it `validation`.

```
var pluginName = "validation"
```

7. The next step is to define our defaults. As we are already defining a lot of our settings inside the HTML, there are not many settings we need to actually configure using JavaScript. The one setting that would be useful for configuring is what HTML should be displayed to show an error message. For this, we will allow the developer using the plugin to provide a template; a default template will be stored in the default settings. To allow the error message to be displayed in the template, we will insert `%E%` where the error message should be outputted:

```
var pluginName = "validation",
  defaults = {
    errorTemplate: '<p class="error">%E%</p>'
  };
```

8. Before we move on to the `init` section of our plugin, we will spend some time writing some basic validators. These will be private and inaccessible outside of the plugin. To start with, we will set up a new object literal called `validators` that we will place after the `Plugin.prototype` object.

```
var validators = {
}
```

9. We will add a series of basic validation methods to this object, for those criteria that are required such as `email` and `phone`. Each validation method will accept an object literal as a parameter, as seen in the following code snippet:

```
var validators = {
   required: function(validationAttr){

   },
   email: function(validationAttr){

   },
   phone: function(validationAttr){

   }
};
```

10. Starting with the `required` method, we need to check that its value is not `null`, that it is not an empty string, and that the value does not equal the default value. This is accomplished by the following code:

```
required: function(validationAttr){
   var valid = true;

   if (validationAttr.value === null || validationAttr.value
     === '') {
     valid = false;
   }

   return valid;
},
```

11. Moving on to the e-mail validation, we need to use a regular expression to validate that the value added is in fact an e-mail address. To test the regular expression, we will use `.match`, as shown:

```
email: function(validationAttr){
   var valid = false;
```

```
    if (validationAttr.value.match(/^((?:(?:(?:\w[\.\-\+]?)*)\w)+)\@
((?:(?:(?:\w[\.\-\+]?){0,62})\w)+)\.(\w{2,6})$/)) {
      valid = true;
    }

    return valid;
  },
```

12. The final validation method is for phone validation. We will use a regular expression to validate the phone number. To test the regular expression, we will use `.match`, as shown:

```
phone: function(validationAttr){
  var valid = false;

  if (validationAttr.value.match(/^(0(\d|\s){8,12}$)|(\+(\d|\s)
{8,12}$)/)) {
      valid = true;
  }

  return valid;
}
```

13. We can now move on to the `init` section of our plugin. To validate the form, we need to handle two types of events, the submission of the form and the changing of the value of the form element. The prerequisite for our plugin to work is that it should be applied to the form element; we can then use event delegation to add the two types of events directly to the form. We will pass three parameters to the `jQuery.on()` method, firstly the event, secondly the selector, and finally the event handler method that we will shortly be adding to our prototype object. For the `change` event, we will use `[data-validate]` as the selector, which will select any form element that we have added validation to. For the form submission, we will add a `submit` event to the form., as shown:

```
init: function() {
  $(this.element).on('change','[data-validate]',this.
validateField);
  $(this.element).on('submit',this.validateForm);
},
```

14. The next step is to set up our methods, the first being `validateForm` and the second, `validateField`. The `validateForm` method will accept the jQuery event object as its only parameter and the `validateField` method will take the jQuery event object and a parameter called `that`. The code snippet for this is as follows:

```
Plugin.prototype = {
  init: function() {
```

```
    $(this.element).on('change','[data-validate]',this.
validateField);
    $(this.element).on('click',this.validateForm);
  },
  validateForm: function(e){

  },
  validateField: function(e,that){

  }
};
```

15. The first method we will get started with is the `validateField` method that will validate any field. When we added the `validateForm` method to `Plugin. prototype`, you may have noticed that we pass two parameters to the method. The first parameter is the jQuery object that is passed to the method by jQuery. The second parameter is an optional parameter called `that` (a pseudonym for `this` used where `validateField` is called in a way that makes `this` have an incorrect scope).

16. At the start of the `validateField` method, we will setup several different variables:

   - `valid`: The `valid` variable keeps track of whether the field is valid or not.

   - `field`: The `field` variable defaults to equaling `that`. If `that` were not passed to the method as a parameter, the field becomes equal to `this`.

   - `$field`: Once we have decided whether the `field` attribute is equal to `that` or `this`, we will get the jQuery object of the `field` attribute and store it as `$field`.

   - `requiredValidators`: The `requiredValidators` variable stores an array of validators required to be executed on the form field. This is retrieved from the `data-validate` data attribute using `.attr('data-validate')` and then splitting it into an array using `.split(' ')`.

   - `plugin`: The `plugin` variable stores the current instance of the plugin retrieved using `$(e.delegateTarget).data("plugin_" + pluginName)`.

   - `$error`: Any existing error message for a field will have their jQuery object cached using `jQuery.data()`. These can then be retrieved and removed.

   - `errorHTML`: The `errorHTML` will be used for building up the error message's HTML page.

```
validateField: function(e,that){
  var valid = true,
  field = that || this,
  $field = $(field),
  requiredValidators = $field.attr('data-validate').split('
    '),
  plugin = $(e.delegateTarget).data("plugin_" +
    pluginName),
  $error = $field.data('error') || null,
  errorHTML = null;
}
```

17. After setting up our variables, we can now remove any existing error messages, as shown in the following code snippet:

```
validateField: function(e,that){
  var valid = true,
  field = that || this,
  $field = $(field),
  requiredValidators = $field.attr('data-validate').split('
    '),
  plugin = $(e.delegateTarget).data("plugin_" +
    pluginName),
  $error = $field.data('error') || null,
  errorHTML = null;

  if($error !== null){
    $error.remove();
  }
}
```

18. Now that we have removed any existing error messages, we can start with validating the field. The first step in validating the field is to set up the `validationAttr` object literal with the value of the element. The code to achieve this is as follows:

```
validateField: function(e,that){
  var valid = true,
    field = that || this,
    $field = $(field),
    requiredValidators = $field.attr('data-validate').split(' '),
    plugin = $(e.delegateTarget).data("plugin_" +
      pluginName),
    $error = $field.data('error') || null,
    errorHTML = null;
```

```
    if($error !== null){
      $error.remove();
    }

    var validationAttr = {
      value: $field.val()
    };
  }
```

19. We now need to go through each of the items in the `requiredValidators` array and run each of the validators. We will use a `for` loop to go through the array of `requiredValidators` as shown:

```
validateField: function(e,that){
  var valid = true,
    field = that || this,
    $field = $(field),
    requiredValidators = $field.attr('data-validate').split(' '),
    plugin = $(e.delegateTarget).data("plugin_" +
      pluginName),
    $error = $field.data('error') || null,
    errorHTML = null;

  if($error !== null){
    $error.remove();
  }

  var validationAttr = {
    value: $field.val()
  };

  for (var i = 0; i < requiredValidators.length; i++) {
  }
}
```

20. Inside the `for` loop, we now need to run the correct validation. We can do this by running `validators[requiredValidators[i]](validationAttr)`. Breaking down this statement, we find that the `validators[requiredValidators[i]]` part of the code selects the method and the `(validationAttr)` part executes the method with the `validation` attributes object as the parameter. The `validation` method is executed as a part of an `if` statement. If the validation fails, it will execute the code required to set the failed state. This can be understood better by the following code snippet:

```
validateField: function(e,that){
  var valid = true,
    field = that || this,
    $field = $(field),
```

```
        requiredValidators = $field.attr('data-validate').split(' '),
        plugin = $(e.delegateTarget).data("plugin_" +
          pluginName),
        $error = $field.data('error') || null,
        errorHTML = null;

    if($error !== null){
      $error.remove();
    }

    var validationAttr = {
      value: $field.val()
    };

    for (var i = 0; i < requiredValidators.length; i++) {

      if(validators[requiredValidators[i]](validationAttr)
        === false){


      }
    }
}
```

21. We now need to handle what happens if the validation fails. Inside our `if` statement, we need to add the functionality to show an error message. The error message needs to use the error message template that we defined in the template combined with the text for the error message, which is defined on the field as a data attribute. To do this, we need to set the `errorHTML` variable to the value returned by using JavaScript's `.replace()` on `plugin.options.errorTemplate` to replace `%E%` with the value of the current validators, error message.

22. We then need to append the error message to the page; simultaneously, we also want to cache the error element jQuery object. We can do this all in one line of code by using the `jQuery.data` method to store an error on the field. As the value of the data we are adding, we can use `$(errorHTML).insertAfter($field)` that returns the error message of the corresponding jQuery object, which is now cached using `.data()`.

23. Finally, before we close our `if` statement, we can set `valid` equal to `false` and break out of our loop using `break`. The code snippet for this purpose is as follows:

```
validateField: function(e,that){
  var valid = true,
    field = that || this,
    $field = $(field),
    requiredValidators = $field.attr('data-validate').split(' '),
    plugin = $(e.delegateTarget).data("plugin_" +
      pluginName),
    $error = $field.data('error') || null,
    errorHTML = null;

  if($error !== null){
    $error.remove();
  }

  var validationAttr = {
    value: $field.val()
  };

  for (var i = 0; i < requiredValidators.length; i++) {

    if(validators[requiredValidators[i]](validationAttr)
      === false){
      errorHTML =
        plugin.options.errorTemplate.replace("%E%",
          $field.attr('data-'+requiredValidators[i]));
      $field.data('error',$(errorHTML).insertAfter($field));

      valid = false;
      break;
    }
  }

  return valid;
}
```

24. At this point, our elements on change functionality should be working; however, the next step is to add the functionality for when the form is submitted.

25. We can now get started with adding the functionality to the `validateForm` method. The first step is to define our variables. For this method, we will need a simple Boolean variable named `valid`, and a plugin variable that we will load the plugin instance into.

```
validateForm: function(e){
  var valid = true,
    plugin = $(this).data("plugin_" + pluginName);
},
```

26. Our next step is to go through the form looking for elements we want to validate. We will do this by finding elements with the `data-validate` attribute set and then use `jQuery.each()` to loop through each of these, as shown in the following code snippet:

```
validateForm: function(e){
  var valid = true,
    plugin = $(this).data("plugin_" + pluginName);
  $(plugin.element).find('[data-validate]').each(function(){
  });
},
```

27. Now that we are looping through our fields, we can add some validation rather than duplicate the change validation, which we have already written. We will simply use an `if` statement to check the result of the `validateField` method on each element. If at any point the `validateField` method returns the value as `false`, we set `valid` equal to `false` as the form has failed validation.

```
validateForm: function(e){
  var valid = true, plugin = $(this).data("plugin_" + pluginName);

  $(plugin.element).find('[data-validate]').each(function(){
    if(plugin.validateField(e,this) === false){
      valid = false;
    }
  });
},
```

28. Our final step is to return the `valid` variable.

```
validateForm: function(e){
  var valid = true, plugin = $(this).data("plugin_" +
    pluginName);

  $(plugin.element).find('[data-validate]').each(function(){
    if(plugin.validateField(e,this) === false){
      valid = false;
    }
  });

  return valid;
},
```

There's more...

It is important that our validators work as we expect and that, if we go on to improve our plugin by adding extra validators, we should perform a regression test on our code. While we could manually test each of our validation methods, it makes sense to write some unit tests to test the code.

Unfortunately our plugin isn't quite ready for unit testing as our validators are nested within a closure and we are therefore unable to call them directly.

1. The first step is for us to add a new method to our plugin prototype, which will act as a pass-through for our tests. This method needs to be minimal as we don't want to be testing the pass through; we want to test the actual validator. We will call our new method `validateString`, and it will simply take the options passed to the plugin and perform the validation. As the validators expect to receive an object literal, we will setup the object literal with the value. We then simply return the value returned by the validator, as shown in the following code snippet:

```
validateString: function(options){
  var validationAttr = {
    value: options.val
  };
  return validators[options.validator](validationAttr);
}
```

2. With our new method complete, we now need to update the plugin wrapper to add support for calling the `validateString` method. We will need to add an `if` statement to determine whether the plugin should run as normal or whether it is being used to simply validate a string.

```
$.fn[pluginName] = function ( options, methodOptions) {
  var localPlugin = null;

  if (options === undefined || typeof options ===
    'object') {
    return this.each(function () {
      if (!$.data(this, "plugin_" + pluginName)) {
        $.data(this, "plugin_" + pluginName, new Plugin( this,
options ));
      }
    });
  }
  else if(options === "validateString"){
    localPlugin = new Plugin( null, {} );
    return localPlugin.validateString(methodOptions);
  }
};
```

3. Now that we have updated our plugin, we can test this out in the browser console. Once you have the page open and have opened the console, you can test the new version of the plugin with:

```
$().validation('validateString',{val: "test", validator:
"required"});
```

4. This should simply return `true` to the console.

5. Now that we are happy that our changes to our plugin are working, we will start setting up QUnit. The first step is to create a new HTML file called `test.html`, which will be used for our unit tests. We will use the QUnit CSS and JavaScript both directly from the jQuery site, so the only extra file we need to create is the `test.js` file that will house our tests.

```
<!DOCTYPE html>
<html>
  <head>
    <title></title>
    <link rel="stylesheet" href="http://code.jquery.com/qunit/
qunit-1.11.0.css">
  </head>
  <body>
    <div id="qunit"></div>
    <div id="qunit-fixture"></div>

    <script src="js/vendor/jquery-1.9.1.min.js"></script>
    <script src="js/plugin.js"></script>
    <script src="http://code.jquery.com/qunit/qunit-1.11.0.js"></
      script>
    <script src="js/tests.js"></script>
  </body>
</html>
```

6. The next step is our `tests.js` file. There are three main test cases we want to create, the first to test the required validation, the second to test the e-mail validation, and the third to test the phone number validation.

7. Starting with the required validation test case, our first step is to create our test case. This is done by executing the test method with two properties. The first is the name of the test case, and the second is a callback method where we will add all the individual assertions:

```
test( "Required validation", function() {
});
```

8. When adding our assertions, we are going to use the `ok` method to which we will pass two parameters. The first is our condition and the second is the name of the individual assertion. For the `condition` parameter, we will simply check that the plugin validation method is returning what we expect; in our case, the values will equal `true` or `false`. For our first assertion, we will set the value to `""`, and we expect that this will return `false` as it is an empty string; for our second assertion, we will pass `Required value`, and we expect that this will return `true` as it is a populated value:

```
test( "Required validation", function() {
  ok($().validation('validateString',{val: "", validator:
    "required"}) === false, "Value is not entered");
  ok($().validation('validateString',{val: "Required
    value", validator: "required"}) === true, "Value is
      entered");
});
```

9. The next step is to do the same for the e-mail validation: for our first assertion we will set the value to `hello` and we expect that this will return `false` as it is not a valid e-mail address; for our second assertion, we will pass `hello@example.com`, and we expect that this will return `true` as it is a valid e-mail address.

```
test( "Email Validation", function() {
  ok($().validation('validateString',{val: "hello", validator:
    "email"}) === false, "Value is not email address");
  ok($().validation('validateString',{val: "hello@example.com",
    validator: "email"}) === true, "Value is email address");
});
```

10. Finally we will add our test case for the phone number validation, for our first assertion we will set the value to "hello" and we expect that this will return false as it is not a valid phone number, for our second assertion we will pass "01234789777" and we expect that this will return true as it is a phone number.

```
test( "Phone Number Validation", function() {
  ok($().validation('validateString',{val: "hello", validator:
    "phone"}) === false, "Value is not phone number");
  ok($().validation('validateString',{val: "01234789777",
    validator: "phone"}) === true, "Value is a phone number");
});
```

11. Upon opening this in the browser, we will be presented with the tests; if you look at each test case you will notice `(0,2,2)`. These values indicate there were zero failures, two passes out of a total of two assertions.

To help you with your own plugin development, you should take advantage of the many resources available on the Web.

jQuery plugins documentation

The official documentation for information about jQuery Plugins can be found at: `http://learn.jquery.com/plugins/`

GitHub help

Information about how to use GitHub is available at `https://help.github.com/`.

JonathanFielding.com

My blog that has tutorials, jQuery plugins, and a portfolio of my work: `http://www.jonathanfielding.com`.

Thank you for buying
Instant jQuery Boilerplate for Plugins

About Packt Publishing

Packt, pronounced 'packed', published its first book "*Mastering phpMyAdmin for Effective MySQL Management*" in April 2004 and subsequently continued to specialize in publishing highly focused books on specific technologies and solutions.

Our books and publications share the experiences of your fellow IT professionals in adapting and customizing today's systems, applications, and frameworks. Our solution based books give you the knowledge and power to customize the software and technologies you're using to get the job done. Packt books are more specific and less general than the IT books you have seen in the past. Our unique business model allows us to bring you more focused information, giving you more of what you need to know, and less of what you don't.

Packt is a modern, yet unique publishing company, which focuses on producing quality, cutting-edge books for communities of developers, administrators, and newbies alike. For more information, please visit our website: www.packtpub.com.

Writing for Packt

We welcome all inquiries from people who are interested in authoring. Book proposals should be sent to author@packtpub.com. If your book idea is still at an early stage and you would like to discuss it first before writing a formal book proposal, contact us; one of our commissioning editors will get in touch with you.

We're not just looking for published authors; if you have strong technical skills but no writing experience, our experienced editors can help you develop a writing career, or simply get some additional reward for your expertise.

jQuery 1.4 Reference Guide

A comprehensive exploration of the popular JavaScript library

jQuery 1.4 Reference Guide

ISBN: 978-1-849510-04-2   Paperback: 336 pages

A comprehensive exploration of the popular JavaScript library

1. Quickly look up features of the jQuery library

2. Step through each function, method, and selector expression in the jQuery library with an easy-to-follow approach

3. Understand the anatomy of a jQuery script

4. Write your own plug-ins using jQuery's powerful plug-in architecture

jQuery Plugin Development

Beginner's Guide

jQuery Plugin Development Beginner's Guide

ISBN: 978-1-849512-24-4   Paperback: 288 pages

Build powerful, interactive plugi-ins to implement jquery to its best

1. Utilize jQuery's plugin framework to create a wide range of useful jQuery plugins from scratch

2. Understand development patterns and best practices and move up the ladder to master plugin development

3. Discover the ins and outs of some of the most popular jQuery plugins in action

4. A Beginner's Guide packed with examples and step-by-step instructions to quickly get your hands dirty in developing high quality jQuery plugins

Please check **www.PacktPub.com** for information on our titles

jQuery Mobile Web Development Essentials

ISBN: 978-1-849517-26-3   Paperback: 246 pages

Learn to use the touch-optimized, cross-device, cross-platform jQM web framework for smartphones and tablets

1. Create websites that work beautifully on a wide range of mobile devices with jQuery mobile

2. Learn to prepare your jQuery mobile project by learning through three sample applications

3. Packed with easy to follow examples and clear explanations of how to easily build mobile-optimized websites

jQuery Tools UI Library

ISBN: 978-1-849517-80-5   Paperback: 112 pages

Learn jQuery Tools with clear, practical examples and get inspiration for developing your own ideas with the library

1. Learn how to use jQuery Tools, with clear, practical projects that you can use today in your websites

2. Learn how to use useful tools such as Overlay, Scrollable, Tabs and Tooltips

3. Full of practical examples and illustrations, with code that you can use in your own projects, straight from the book

Please check **www.PacktPub.com** for information on our titles